D1000680

FEW AND

FAR BETWEEN

FEW AND

FAR BETWEEN

Moments in the

North American

Desert

PHOTOGRAPHS AND TEXT
BY JOHN MARTIN CAMPBELL

FOREWORD
BY TONY HILLERMAN

MUSEUM OF NEW MEXICO PRESS
SANTA FE

508.3154
C188

FOR
ROSEMARY TALLEY
MARSHA F. JACKSON
AND LORNA DEMPSEY

Copyright © 1997 John Martin Campbell. *All rights reserved*. No part of this book may be reproduced in any form or by any means whatsoever without the expressed written consent of the publisher.

Manufactured in Korea

Project editor: Mary Wachs

Design and production: David Skolkin

Composition: Set in Cochin with Futura display.

Page 143 from the collections of the Museum of New Mexico, Santa Fe. Page 147 from the collections of the U.S. National Museum, New York.

Library of Congress Cataloging-in-Publication Data available.

10 9 8 7 6 5 4 3 2 1

Map on page xii after Brown (1982), Dick-Peddie (1993), Fiero (1986), Larson (1977), MacMahon (1985), McGinnies (1977), Olin (1977), and the author's field studies.

MUSEUM OF NEW MEXICO PRESS
POST OFFICE BOX 2087
SANTA FE, NEW MEXICO 87504

CONTENTS

FOREWORD

Tony Hillerman

JACK CAMPBELL'S photographs, and their accompanying text, speak eloquently of the desert country, but in one sense these remarkable black-and-white images tell us as much about the artist as they do of the arid and empty landscape that calls him. In the space I have here, I will try to cast a bit of light on what this book doesn't cover—the man who decided what he should show us to help us understand this land of vast empty spaces and very little rain.

How can a person who has known "Anthropology Jack Campbell" for thirty years come to think of him as a photographer? I met him first as a fellow member of the University of New Mexico faculty. Then, when I began trying to write my own books he became a helpful authority on Southwest tribal cultures. Soon he was a friend and fellow poker player. Only much later did I come to know him as his fellow anthropologists do—as an internationally recognized authority on the frozen world above the Arctic Circle.

I first crossed paths with Jack Campbell when a professor in my department, aware that I had a lot to learn about teaching, pointed to him as a master of that game. He suggested I sit in on some of Campbell's lectures. I did, and watched him mesmerize a class of freshman with a description of how the ebb and flow of snowshoe rabbit and other animal populations in the subarctic affected not just the foxes, wolves, and eagles of the far north but the culture of the people who developed their society in that hostile landscape up toward the Bering Sea. In that course, he taught his students how to see the details that matter. In this book of his photographs he does the same for all of us.

He shows us, for example, not just a creosotebush but its peculiar setting—the isolation from competition that allows it to live where rain rarely falls and drains quickly away. He shows us a cluster of agave, probably planted by Stone Age farmers, that makes us understand that the right plant can endure long after its human planters die away. He shows us the vast emptiness of basin-and-range topography and includes the great sky to tell us as much about its nature as the land itself. Turn the pages and look down a row of crooked fence posts stretching across white flatness. The photograph is of a wet playa, but it also illustrates how total desolation can have a sort of stark beauty that lifts the spirit. Flip to another page for an illustration of the ocotillo, which provides framing material for the wikiups of the Seri Indians. But you also notice the drifted sand held by its roots and its barren, wind-bent stems. Thus, you learn something of the Seri people who found a way for our species to live where few plants survive.

Enough of this. Turn the page. Someone who is both an artist and a teacher will show you the desert as he sees it through his camera lens.

PREFACE

THIS BOOK HAD ITS BEGINNINGS in the 1930s. Our farm occupied land that had been reclaimed from the big sage barrens of eastern Washington. From our place westward there were other irrigated farms and then the Cascade Mountains, but eastward the desert lay barely out the door. For a fourth grader it was a ten-minute walk to a sagebrush bench on the west bank of the Yakima River, and across on the east side there was sagebrush as far as you could see. East of the Yakima the desert rolled up between two ridges to a horizon 20 miles away, beyond which it was 10 miles to the Columbia River. Across the Columbia, in the direction of Idaho, there was desert for another 70 miles.

Except on foot or horseback there was no direct way to get through the stretch of dry country between our house and the Columbia. And thus protected was a rolling, treeless landscape of basaltic canyons and native plants and animals that inspired me to a career in natural history. Then there were the Wanapums.

On the eastern edge of this wild tract the Columbia ran down for several miles over bedrock reefs in a cataract known as Priest Rapids. The rapids concentrated salmon on their way to upriver spawning grounds, and because of the resultant good fishing—as well as the isolation of the place—a band of American Indians, the Wanapums, lived at the rapids on our side of the Columbia. The Wanapums were close kin to other northwestern interior Indians, but they were reclusive and old-fashioned. They had refused to live on a reservation, and hidden out in the desert they practiced a native revivalist religion whose followers were known as Shakers (not the same as the British and American Shakers of the eighteenth and nineteenth centuries).

I saw the Wanapums first when I was in the sixth grade. My father was both a farmer and the superintendent of Selah Consolidated Schools, whose district covered some 400 square miles, mainly uninhabited sagebrush, and whose last remaining one-room schoolhouse stood at the foot of Priest Rapids a few miles downstream from the Indian camp. Priest Rapids School was maintained most specifically for the children of a half dozen white families, the operators of a little power plant whose electricity was wired down the Columbia. Still, the school was meant to serve any child in the region, and in that regard the Wanapums had become a bureaucratic embarrassment. Their encampment of forty-five or fifty men, women, and children lay within the Selah district, but in violation of the law the Wanapum children had not been attending school.

Neither my father nor the county superintendent, a Mr. Van Horn, held much hope of getting the Indians to the schoolhouse. Nevertheless, an effort was required and I got to go along. To get there we had to drive 100 miles around, 90 of which were over unpaved roads. We reached the camp through a sagebrush plain upon which, as I remember vividly, grazed hundreds of Indian horses. As anticipated, our mission failed. Johnny Buck, the spiritual and secular leader of the band, told us simply that the children didn't want to go to school, and with that the school-house–Wanapum issue was swept under the bureaucratic rug.

But meanwhile I had gotten a glimpse of what to me was an astonishing way of life. Seasonally, the Wanapums were itinerant pickers of the white man's hops and apples, but home was beside Priest Rapids. The numbers of their saddle horses when compared with the population of the Indian band harkened back to the golden years of the middle nineteenth century. Their houses were of an old design, framed in whittled poles and covered with reed mats. And as I learned later on, they buried their dead in unmarked rock-slide graves, used vessels of ground stone, and navigated the rapids in a canoe carved from a big tree that years earlier had come down the river on flood. So to a sixth grader the Wanapums were fascinating, wild Indians, and my career plans were given further direction.

I am describing the Columbia Basin as it was before the big water and power projects came on line—Grand Coulee, Potholes, Priest Rapids and Rosa—when 24,000 square miles of eastern Washington were dry. Go back another fifty years to the 1880s, the end of the Indian Wars and the first irrigation ditches, and you can add another few hundred sections. But in 1938, and for nearly two decades afterward, most of the eastern part of the state had been desert for upward of eight thousand years.

In the 1950s the Wanapums were flooded out and dispersed by construction of the Priest Rapids Dam, and over the intervening decades nearly all of the old Washington sagebrush country has come under irrigation. Worth noting, however, given our present concerns with preser-

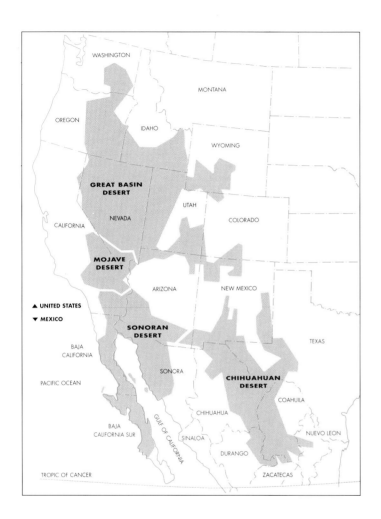

vation, are the curious circumstances by which has been preserved that wild tract lying between the Yakima and Columbia rivers. Soon after the Japanese bombed Pearl Harbor, an American artillery captain came looking for a place where the biggest field guns in the U.S. arsenal could be fired in any direction without killing anything bigger than a coyote. And until today this military post, off-limits to all but artillery and armored cavalry, shelters an array of desert plants and animals, not least among them being the last viable population of sage grouse in Washington State—courtesy of the U.S. Army.

As things turned out, I chose a career in anthropology, but with the idea that I would remain an amateur in the biological and earth sciences. The following pictures and texts reflect that accommodation. My objective for this book is twofold: First, to describe the natural history of the North American Desert; and second, with an emphasis on aboriginal food-getting, to explain how, in ancient times, human intellect related to the desert's various environments, which together span from central Mexico to the Canadian border.

From 1986 to 1996, inclusive, the search for appropriate photographs involved more than 400,000 miles of road travel through all of the desert's major regions. Those journeys resulted in a body of pictures, a selection of which appears in the following pages. These plates are enlarged from 4×5-inch Kodak Plus-X, Tri-X, and Ektachrome E100S film exposed in Kodak and Calumet large-format view cameras. Black-and-white photo printing is by Hugh N. Stratford.

Textual descriptions and interpretations derive from the literature, discussions with students and colleagues in anthropology, biology, and the earth sciences, and personal field observations. Two scholars were most instrumental in the production of this book. Katherine K-S Kallestad, critic and archival helpmate, and Marjorie Kilberg Shea, naturalist and field associate on numerous desert expeditions. Contributors to whom I extend special thanks include John P. Hubbard, Peter M. Whiteley, and Thomas C. Windes. Others are Keith Basso, Clifford S. Crawford, Mary Kay Day, Eva Freimuth, Richard W. Geist, Tom and Donna Grissom, John W. Hawley, Lucile Housley, Becky Johnston, Walter Ballad Johnston, Marie C. Lakits, Spencer R. Luke, William C. Martin, W. Bruce Mathews, Ramiro Matos, John M. Montagne, Thomas H. Morris, Mary Beck Mosher, Patricia L. Nietfeld, David Grant Noble, David H. Nufer, Robert W. Parker, Stephen C. Porter, Loren D. Potter, Polly Schaafsma, Robert R. Sluss, Dennis J. Stanford, Louise I. Stiver, Thom Tennies, Janet A. Thomas, Alan J. VerPloeg, Curt A. Wiberg, and Wirt H. Wills. And thanks to Mary Wachs. No writer could wish for a more sympathetic, enthusiastic, and expert editor.

Desert pavement may result
from one of at least three
mechanical factors, but the
most impressive examples
seem to be caused by freezing,
thawing, and shrinking of
damp, porous soils, a process
that forces small, flat stones to
the surface. Harney County,
Oregon, 1996.

ORIGINS

THE NORTH AMERICAN DESERT extends irregularly from east-central Washington to the Mexican state of Zacatecas and from the Big Bend of the Rio Grande in Texas to the Pacific beaches of Baja California Sur. It covers something on the order of 500,000 square miles, and practically speaking you can travel from one end of it to the other without running out of desert. Biologists split it into four parts: the Great Basin, Chihuahuan, and Sonoran deserts, the big ones, and last the Mojave, squeezed between the Great Basin and the Sonoran.

A desert, with its pronounced aridity, few trees, and eroded ground surfaces, is as unmistakable as any landscape on earth, but still there is no general agreement on how a desert ought to be defined. In all definitions, lack of precipitation is the single common factor, but how to apply lack of rain, or snow, is a subject for argument. A recent and perhaps the present most popular equation has it that a region is a desert when its moisture loss from evapotranspiration (combined ground surface evaporation and plant transpiration) exceeds its total annual precipitation. But meanwhile, the traditional geographer's definition—and the one used in this book—says that when a stretch of land gets less than ten inches of average annual precipitation, then that region is a desert. This old yardstick is not precise, but most parts of every desert on earth get less than ten inches a year, which makes it as good a working definition as any.

If one counts the Arctic and Antarctic, 30 percent of the earth's land surfaces is covered

by desert. Leaving out the incredibly dry polar regions, and depending upon how you split them up, there remain thirteen to seventeen very large deserts. And using the smaller figure, lumping rather than splitting, they are distributed as follows: Africa has three; Asia, six; Australia, one; North America, one; and South America, two. Among these, the largest by far is the Sahara in North Africa, with 3.5 million square miles. The North American is fifth in size.

Deserts result from both natural causes and human meddling. Within the historic period, and especially within the past century, deserts have grown, encroaching upon and consuming neighboring semidesert grasslands. In part this is a reflection of naturally increasing aridity over the past several thousand years, a phenomenon science has yet to explain.

Shown here is the hard surface of a typical dry playa, with saltbushes in the foreground. Millard County, Utah, 1996.

But many of these desert encroachments result from domestic grazing and farming. Agronomists estimate that around the world, 40 square miles per day become desert. This adds up to 14,600 square miles of new desert each year, converted from marginal countryside by livestock, dry farming, and, surprisingly perhaps, irrigation.

Overgrazing and dry farming remove native ground cover, exposing it to the forces of wind and drought. Irrigation takes its toll in a number of ways. First, the extraordinarily high evaporation rate in arid and semiarid regions requires enormous quantities of water which, as with evaporation, often impregnates the surface with salts, thus ruining the ground for farming. This is true even when the mineral content of the water is not high. Second, pouring water on much dryland soil has the effect of raising and concentrating salts already present in the ground. And third, modern pumping techniques allow the tapping of underground reservoirs filled thousands of years ago during pluvial (wet) times but which are no longer being replenished. The Ogallala Aquifer in the central and southern Great Plains is but one of many examples. The Ogallala presently irrigates fifteen million acres of agriculture, but these domestic crops have replaced wild, thin prairie sod, and when the reservoir runs dry the plowed fields will turn to desert.

Still, deserts (excluding the polar zones) derive principally from one or a combination of five natural, rather than human, factors, and to one degree or another the North American results from all five of them. Two have to do with the dual effects of the horse latitudes, with their trade winds, and the Tropics of Cancer and Capricorn. Most deserts lie on or near the Tropic of Cancer, which girdles the earth about 23.5 degrees north of the equator, or on or near the Tropic of Capricorn, which circles at an equal distance south. In summer the sun stands directly over Cancer, in winter directly over Capricorn, thereby at different times of the year

subjecting each of them—and their neighboring regions—to direct, intense solar radiation. The Tropic of Cancer misses our desert by only a few miles, which largely explains the searing summer heat of its southern reaches.

A second cause is the movement of tropical and subtropical air. Very warm, equatorial air masses, called trade winds, rise, cool, and condense, producing the torrential monsoon rains of the tropics. These same air masses, now cool and dry, descend across the horse latitudes, areas of calm, where they again become heated and highly absorbent, sucking the moisture from the land, resulting in so-called "horse latitude deserts."

A third natural cause of deserts is that of cold or relatively cold near-shore ocean currents running parallel to continental coasts. Winds blowing landward across these waters are cooled, and their moisture condenses and falls at sea before reaching land. The driest of all deserts, the Peruvian Atacama, results from the north-flowing Humboldt Current, whose origins are in the Antarctic. Similarly, the southwesternmost edge of the North American Desert, the west coast of Baja California, is dry because of the California Current flowing south from the Gulf of Alaska.

Nearly all desert surfaces are subject to continuous wind scouring, a far more constant dryland erosive factor than running water. In this picture the deep roots of arrowweed (*Pulchea servicea*) permit this plant to hang on as the desert floor becomes increasingly deflated. Inyo County, California, 1996.

The fourth factor relates to a region's remoteness from the nearest ocean. Practically all terrestrial water is derived from the seas, and air moisture is likely to condense and fall before reaching far-off interior regions. This holds true especially if the remote interior is relatively high, causing approaching water-bearing clouds to rise, cool, and condense. Parts of the Sahara and parts of some of the Asian deserts are caused by these elements of distance and elevation, as is some of the North American, for example the high-desert sagebrush country of western and central Wyoming.

Composed of sandstones, limestones, shales, and other sedimentary rocks cross-bedded and folded within the past fifteen million years or so, the Bare Mountains are typical of Great Basin topography. Nye County, Nevada, 1996.

But the largest part of the North American is produced by the fifth factor: tall mountain chains, in this case the Cascades and the Sierra Nevada, that block the western interior from the water-laden air of the coast. This "rain-shadow desert," as geographers call the east-lying dry country, has its genesis in the California Current, an ocean river that circles the North Pacific as a Gulf Stream analogue. Curiously, this is the same ocean stream that, because of its relative coldness as it approaches the horse latitudes, results in the desertic Pacific coast of the Baja Peninsula. But farther north, as it flows southward along the Northwest Coast, its water is typically warmer than the air above, and as it vaporizes and rises it is blown shoreward by the prevailing winds, the westerlies. When it reaches the mountains this wet air rises, condenses, and falls, thus creating both the rainy jungles of the coast and the dry barrens eastward.

The single most remarkable of the North American Desert's big landscapes begins here on the eastern foot of the ranges. It is an enormous natural bowl, nearly as large as the rest of our desert areas combined, and it encompasses all of Nevada and substantial parts of neighboring states. John Charles Frémont was neither the first nor the last white man to go thirsty in this great sink lying between the Rockies and the Sierra Nevada, but he was the first to map its boundaries. In 1843, as a brevetted captain, U.S. Army, and with a cartographer, a few retainers, and a remount herd, Frémont set out to reconnoiter this, the last big, unexplored, unreported region of what was to become the forty-eight states.

It took him most of two years. They walked and rode from Wyoming down the Bear River to its mouth in the Great Salt Lake, west across Utah to eastern Oregon, south through eastern California, east across southernmost Nevada, and north along the foot of the Rockies back to the

As its name implies, an alluvial fan is created by running water. The cobbles and boulders shown here were disgorged by desert cloudbursts from the narrow mountain crevice in the background. Inyo County, California, 1996.

Great Salt Lake. Thus they circumnavigated a desert countryside of 220,000 square miles whose waters have no outlet to the ocean; a bowl whose few creeks and rivers sink into the ground or pool and evaporate. Frémont called it the Great Basin, a proper name to this day from which is derived Great Basin Desert, although the latter, as we shall describe, includes dry country lying beyond the basin's borders.

As it exists now, the North American Desert is young. Dating to nine thousand years ago or thereabouts, it is one of a series of deserts which over the past several million years has occupied more or less the same land area and which had its beginnings when the big western mountain chains were created during the Miocene epoch, some twenty million years ago. This present desert's youthfulness results from the wasting away of the most recent of four great "ice ages" which at intervals over the past one million years have covered much of the Northern Hemisphere with glacial ice.

The latest of these, in North America known as the Wisconsin Glacial Stage, was triggered seventy thousand years ago by slight but sustained lowerings of average annual air temperatures. The reasons for those temperature shifts are obscure but their consequences were profound. They caused ice to accumulate on the northwestern cordilleran region, in Alaska and Canada, and on the country near Hudson Bay, from whence the glaciers grew, moved, and coalesced until by eighteen thousand years before Christ ice covered nearly all of northern North America, its glacial front looming south below the Canadian border from Puget Sound east to Vermont.

South of the ice front the coldness of the Wisconsin glacier pushed biotic zones southward and downward. The country lying near the ice evolved either to tundra or steppe, farther south forests moved down from high ground onto what had been open plains, and in the desert most of the low country became lake-filled prairie, savanna, and forest. These several effects of the northern ice permitted snow to pile up in the high country, both on the big mountain chains bordering the desert and on the taller desert ranges, and those snowbanks, lasting over and growing year after year, were transformed eventually into glacial ice. Twenty thousand years ago most of those ice patches covered a few dozen acres of slope; others, a lot of countryside. Such tall desert mountains as Steens, in Oregon, and the Rubys, in Nevada, were covered with hundreds of square miles of glaciers, and farther south, mountain ice caps lay in and near the desert from California to New Mexico.

During summer the meltwater from these desert, or near-desert, glaciers ran either seaward via the big, ancient river systems or poured into the enclosed desert basins. The combined volume of those glacier-fed rivers and creeks was formidable, the more so because their main flows were seasonal and despite the fact that the oceans were being steadily reduced because of the atmospheric water captured in continental ice. Glacial melt, for example, caused the Colorado and the Rio Grande to run seasonally at ten times their present flood stages, and smaller meltwater streams turned desert basins into lakes and seas.

Ancient Lake Bonneville, largest by far of the desert's former lakes, was indeed a sea. When in 1847 the Mormons reached northwest Utah, they found themselves on a narrow strip of sagebrush and saltbush backed on the east by the Wasatch Range and on the west by the Great Salt Lake—all that was left of Bonneville. The Great Salt Lake today is the size of Rhode Island but still only one-eighteenth as big as ancient Lake Bonneville. At its deepest and broadest it covered 20,000 square miles, had a shoreline 3,000 miles long, and was a thousand feet deep. And to this grandeur of lake, stream, and parkland was added a remarkable array of animals: forty-pound trout, condors, straight-horned bison, and woolly mammoths, to name a few, all dwelling in a lush landscape which had been desert for thousands of years before the onset of the Wisconsin.

Such wonders, however, were common across what is now the North American Desert. In New Mexico, for example, there were several Wisconsin Stage lakes, small when compared with Bonneville but great big lakes by present southwestern standards. (Today, New Mexico's largest *natural* lake is three miles long and three feet deep.) Most all of these old, inland freshwater seas have been bone dry for several millennia, but dry as they are some have still an unmistakable look and feel about them.

In Catron County, New Mexico, between Datil and Old Horse Springs, you cross the western beaches of ancient Lake San Agustin. San Agustin, 60 miles long and 150 feet deep, lay beyond the reach of Wisconsin glacial rivers, but like many other landlocked desert lakes it filled because of the increasing wetness of the landscape: from snowmelt, rainwater, and springs now long extinct. San Agustin had its capes, islands, cliffs, and narrows, and both forests and open meadows ran down to its margins.

Now, from the road down to Old Horse Springs—on a threatening, late fall day when the wind is up—you look across 15 miles of saltbush to the old southeast shore and a line of tall, wave-cut bluffs. The bluffs and the hills behind them stand over an alkali desert that used to be the lake floor. But stop your car and get out into the northwest wind and San Agustin comes back. You can smell big water and hear waves pounding in on the sea cliffs.

Then there are the Plains of Estancia, the floor of another Wisconsin Stage lake, lying across the Rio Grande 100 air miles northeast of San Agustin. Lakes Estancia and San Agustin were of about the same size and shape and reached their greatest stands fifteen thousand years ago. Lake Estancia was fed by a few good-sized mountain creeks that tumbled in from the north and west, and big pines and firs grew down to the lake's inlets where the creeks ran in over gravel shoals.

There were cutthroat trout, two or three pounders at least, whose bones have been found in dry clay beds on the lowermost parts of the plains. And with the trout and the big trees there were ospreys nesting in the tall snags above the inlets where in spring the cutthroats came to spawn on the gravel shoals. Here on a spring day, or several of them, if you are patient you may witness one of those mysteries of nature which defy modern scientific enquiry, which may be nothing more than sheer coincidence, but which tantalize and delight us just the same. For while Lake Estancia went dry five thousand years ago, in April during cutthroat spawning time the ospreys come, drifting slowly, searching over the dry, treeless inlets of Estancia.

In these thousands of years when the desert as we know it became transformed, arid-land plants and animals of that most recent pre–Wisconsin Stage desert were pushed into two regions of Mexico that retained desert climatological characteristics. The Wisconsin reached its so-called "maximum" twenty thousand years ago; by ten thousand years ago, in a gradually warming environment, it was finished. Except for mountain glaciers, some of them big and some of which survive today, the Great Ice had melted, and prairies and woods were taking back the old, glaciated land surfaces. Continued climactic warming resulted increasingly in a return of the dry landscapes that in pre-Wisconsin times had occupied the western interior. Those dryland plants and animals that had taken refuge in Mexico spread northward accordingly, thus re-creating, as it were, the North American Desert.

ORIGINS

OVER MOST OF THE GREAT BASIN DESERT, the sagebrush—aromatic, woody, gnarl-trunked—stands serenely dominant. Generally speaking, big sage (*Artemisia tridentata*) grows neither beyond the boundaries of the North American Desert nor within its other subdeserts: the Chihuahuan, Sonoran, and Mojave. Sagebrush is thus an indicator, a signifier. If you are "out in the sagebrush," you are out in the Great Basin Desert.

Waist high, or head high, and spaced out over the ground to make the most of rain and snowmelt, sagebrush is benign, friendly, easy to walk through, easy on the eye. It is thornless. Its leaves are three-toothed—hence, *tridentata*—soft, and battleship gray. An old, weathered big sage may be two hundred years old.

Much of the north american desert results from the rain shadows cast by the Cascades, the Coast Range, and the Sierra Nevada, mountain chains standing various distances east of the Pacific beaches but together creating a tall rampart that runs from British Columbia, and beyond, to Baja California. The California Current—to northwesterners it is the Japanese Current—is part of an oceanic river that circles the North Pacific as a Gulf Stream analogue. Flowing south along the West Coast, its water is commonly warmer than the air above, and as it vaporizes and rises, it is blown onshore by the prevailing westerlies.

Along continental shores prevailing winds blow landward rather than seaward, generally, and the winds of the Northwest Coast are classic examples. To best appreciate them, pick any winter day and walk any beach or headland from Drakes Bay to Cape Flattery. As in this picture, you will feel and see and hear the westerlies.

THE WESTERLIES

LANE COUNTY, OREGON
1988

14

It is a remarkable coast; there is none other like it. Blown shoreward by the westerlies, the moisture-laden air is so wet that its water volume may exceed sixty-five thousand tons per cubic mile of atmosphere. But driven a little farther inland, it is forced upward by the mountains' western walls, where it cools, condenses, and falls on the coastal country, thereby creating the rain forests of the Northwest Coast, the only true jungles of any temperate-zone region on earth. Less than 100 miles eastward, the country lying beyond the mountains, accordingly, is deprived of water.

Even in Washington, "the Evergreen State," the contrast between east and west is astonishing. In part of western Washington, total annual precipitation is 220 inches a year. But eastward across the mountains, east of the big, glacier-covered volcanos and the Cascade crest, annual precipitation is ten inches or so, and one stretch of eastern Washington gets a bare six inches.

THIS PICTURE OF A PACIFIC OCEAN BEACH was made on a balmy midsummer's day in which visibility, nevertheless, was only half a mile. Come here in September and stay until the following June and you will only occasionally get to see the little island off in the distance.

A few yards to our backs stands the rain forest, a forest whose trees are so tall and close growing that sunlight only momentarily, if ever, reaches its floor, where for lack of sun green-leafed plants can hardly grow, and where there are mushrooms that grow nowhere else. It is a gloomy and fascinating place.

THE NORTHWEST COAST

JEFFERSON COUNTY, WASHINGTON

1987

18

Most desert soils are poor. They are thin because little, if any, mulch can accumulate on typical desert ground, and, commonly, they are impregnated with salts. Alkali (salty) flats and basins are hallmarks of the desert, and usually they are so salty that they are barren of vegetation or are colonized only by the most salt-tolerant of plants.

Most such alkaline desert localities are generated naturally by water-borne salts precipitated over long spans of time. But this alkali flat and pond, and many others like it, were created by artificial irrigation. In this case, a depressed flat in shortgrass prairie lands lying some miles beyond the desert's boundaries was flooded by a diversion ditch for the purpose of creating a watering hole. Instead, the inflow raised an abundance of subsurface salts that, as shown here, encrusted and killed standing grasses and reeds and poisoned the water to boot.

ALKALI POND

COLFAX COUNTY, NEW MEXICO
1989

BASIN-AND-RANGE TOPOGRAPHY is landscape distinguished by relatively narrow parallel mountain chains separated by similarly narrow valleys. Much of the desert contains some of this countryside, but the Great Basin of Nevada is classic. Drive, for example, on U.S. 6 southwestward across Nevada from Ely to Tonopah—167 road miles—and you will cross one after another basin and range, their long axes lying north and south.

The ranges were created during the Miocene epoch twenty million years ago and run from 20 or 30 to well over 100 miles in length, but they and their accompanying basins are seldom more than 15 or 20 miles wide. In his *Basin and Range*, John McPhee writes that the ranges remind him of the U.S. Pacific Fleet awaiting the signal to sail against Japan. From thirty-five thousand feet, on Delta Flight 1630 from Reno to Salt Lake City, if you squint your eyes a little you can actually see the ships.

BASIN AND RANGE

WHITE PINE COUNTY, NEVADA
1986

CREATED TWENTY MILLION YEARS AGO, the Sierra Nevada is one of several far western mountain chains which, in turn, created much of the desert. Tall desert ranges contain successive altitudinal belts of vegetation whose species differ noticeably both from one zone to the next and from the plants of the neighboring desert floors.

Mountains catch moisture, and for most of the North American Desert the rough but useful formula is that for each 200-foot vertical gain in altitude there is a one-inch gain in average annual precipitation. Decreasing average annual air temperatures, which mean shorter growing seasons, follow along.

These combined factors result in a total of five major zones in the several thousand vertical feet that reach from the desert floor to the summit ridges shown in this picture. And these zones provide, accordingly, a variety of wild food sources exploited from season to season by such wide-ranging desert vertebrates as mule deer and people.

THE SIERRA NEVADA

INYO COUNTY, CALIFORNIA
1987

THERE IS NOT A MORE ABRUPT and spectacular passage from desert to dense forest than here in the gorge of the Columbia. This is where the river cuts through the Cascade Range to the North Pacific. The view is downriver toward the sea, and westward from this place the Douglas firs, whose branch tips appear in this picture, become veritable giants, 250 feet tall and more, accompanied by great hemlocks, cedars, and spruces.

But upriver for 300 miles there are no bordering forests of any kind, let alone the rain jungles of the Northwest Coast. Instead, east and north from here the river runs through a dry sagebrush desert created by the rain shadow of the Cascades. While over the past fifty years, especially, these two grand life zones with their giant trees and rolling native prairies have been altered radically, with perseverance you can find, still, some of their wonders.

THE GATES OF THE COLUMBIA

HOOD RIVER COUNTY, OREGON

1996

Eastern Washington and adjacent parts of Idaho and Oregon are underlain by 200,000 square miles of basaltic lava, a bedrock basement more than six thousand feet thick. Laid down during the late Miocene and early Pliocene, roughly five million years ago, it subsided and tipped southwestward, thus creating the Columbia Basin and permitting the Columbia River to run to the sea.

Since then, the basin has been covered successively with soils of one kind or another, but this soil mantle is thin, and scarps and outcrops of bedrock stand in every direction. In much of eastern Washington the low outcrops seem to stretch forever, which is why these old desert lands are known unhappily as "scabrock country." More pleasing to the eye are scattered ramparts of columnar basalt, created five million years ago when magma (liquid rock), spewing out aboveground, cooled, solidified, and contracted. Frequently, as in this picture, the elegant columns are hexagonal in cross section.

COLUMNAR BASALT

Yakima County, Washington
1993

Bajadas, the big apronlike rocky slopes of the southern desert, are unmistakable hallmarks of dry desert landscapes, but you have to stand back to appreciate their majestic character. Their lowermost margins along the sides of basin floors may be 10 or 20 miles across; stand too close and you lose the perspective.

Bajadas wind down the mountains like hardened molasses, great slopes of rock rubble, carried by gravity and water, that surround and leave behind, for a time, outlying hills that stand in their way. They are reminiscent of big, slow-moving mountain glaciers, and they are glaciers of sorts. In the desert, a bajada is the best example you will find of what geologists call *mass wasting*, the process by which mountains are degraded and leveled over very long spans of time. Given twenty million years or so, the Funeral Mountains shown here will thereby be demolished.

BAJADA

NYE COUNTY, NEVADA

1989

IF YOU DRIVE A STOUT VEHICLE, Steens Mountain is accessible for about six months each year. From its top you get a kaleidoscopic view of the desert's history. A *cirque*, in geologists' terms, is a big bowl carved by a glacier from the top of a mountain ridge. When this cirque (it is two thousand horizontal feet from the photographer's perch to the uppermost background) was filled with ice, there was no such thing as a North American Desert and the countryside surrounding the mountain's base was a green parkland. Summer meltwater, running from under the glaciers on Steens Mountain, contributed to the lushness of the landscape. Then, by 8000 B.C., both the Wisconsin ice sheet and most of the mountain glaciers were gone, and the interior West began its slow process of drying out. Nowadays, if you will turn 60 or 70 degrees to the right of where this picture was taken, you can look five thousand feet straight down to the floor of an exceedingly dry and barren desert.

CIRQUE

HARNEY COUNTY, OREGON
1988

THIS BOULDER-STREWN RIDGE testifies to Wisconsin Glacial Stage ice in south-central Montana. Hundreds of feet thick, the great ice stretched from ocean to ocean across the northern tier of the present-day forty-eight contiguous states and covered most of Alaska and all but a tiny part of Canada. It is the nature of a glacier, as it creeps slowly across a given landscape, to lay waste to the ground, uprooting and carrying along in its front boulders, cobbles, gravels, trees, and anything else that is movable but that cannot, quite literally, get out of the way.

Then, when the climate warms and the glacier melts back from its leading edges, this debris is left behind in big, elongate windrows called "moraines." Note the enormous boulders, together with smaller rocks, which fell here from the melting ice eighteen thousand years ago.

WISCONSIN STAGE MORAINE

SWEET GRASS COUNTY, MONTANA
1987

THE SOUTHERN EDGE OF THE WISCONSIN glacial wall was sinuous, and where it faced low, open ground, ice peninsulas grew out beyond the main front. Twenty thousand years ago, in what was to become the northernmost reach of the Great Basin Desert, one of the peninsulas, the Okanagan Lobe, reached south to the present town of Coulee City, Washington, and pushed the Columbia River eastward from its ancient bed into the scabrock country. Eventually, the Columbia got back into its old channel, leaving behind the Grand Coulee and its Dry Falls.

Dry Falls in the sagebrush is a monument that, among my fourth grade Wonders of the World, ranked second only to Mount Rainier, and it still does. It marks the place where for three thousand years the Columbia plunged over a basaltic scarp in a falls 400 feet tall, 4 miles wide, and forty times the size of Niagara.

DRY FALLS

GRANT COUNTY, WASHINGTON
1987

36

VOLCANISM HAS PRODUCED some of both the oldest and youngest of the desert's major landforms. Many native tribes assigned supernatural origins to volcanic craters and cones or otherwise treated them as extraordinary terrain features. Near the Chihuahuan Desert, for example, one deep crater contains pure salt that for hundreds of years has been respectfully mined by the Zuni, and volcanic cavities have for centuries been used as religious shrines by other southwestern tribes.

This crater in the Mojave Desert may be only about two hundred years old. Almost certainly the Western Shoshone, who occupied this region, had knowledge of its creation, and some of their tribal members may have actually witnessed the explosion, although, unfortunately, their accounts have not come down to us.

VOLCANIC CRATER

INYO COUNTY, CALIFORNIA
1987

No one knows when people first occupied what is now the North American Desert. The earliest confirmed radiocarbon dates cluster at about 9000 B.C., when today's desert was a landscape of grassy prairies, woodlands, and freshwater lakes. Many archaeologists feel that future work will revise these dates backward.

The flat-topped bench in this picture's lower right is a beach created sixteen thousand years ago by the wind-driven waves of ancient Lake Bonneville, of which the Great Salt Lake is but a small, surviving remnant. Sixteen thousand years ago Lake Bonneville had a shoreline 3,000 miles long. Mammoths and giant ground sloths roamed its strands, and the future site of Salt Lake City lay eight hundred feet below its surface. Today, the nearest shore of the Great Salt Lake lies nearly 40 air miles from the strand line shown here, but quite possibly early Americans once hunted and fished along this very beach.

LAKE BONNEVILLE'S OLDEST BEACH

BOX ELDER COUNTY, UTAH

1994

40

THE NORTH AMERICAN DESERT encompasses not only the great, broad, well-known regions of the Chihuahuan, Great Basin, Mojave, and Sonoran but outlying localities as well. These extensions, or some of them, do not appear universally on inclusive maps of the desert, even though they may be starkly desertic and cover thousands of square miles.

Here is one example: If there was ever a classic, barren desert landscape this is it, yet it lies among peculiar Great Basin Desert corridors that run discontinuously from central and southern Utah to southern Colorado and northern New Mexico that are bordered rather closely by densely forested mountains, snow covered much of each year. The soil is so poor here that it supports only white bursage (*Ambrosia dumosa*). The ramparts in the background show the ravages of typical rare desert cloudbursts, and the dappled ground surface results from a recent, brief pelting rain.

DESERT

GRAND COUNTY, UTAH

1988

42

Red and yellow lichens on a rock face in the canyon of the Yakima River, northernmost Great Basin Desert. Kittitas County, Washington, 1996.

GIVEN ITS EXPANSE of 25 degrees of latitude (1,900 miles) and 8 degrees of longitude (800 miles) and its reach from the ocean to high, interior plateaus, it would seem that the desert has little in the way of unifying qualities. When you drive the most direct route from, say, central Washington to the Sonoran coast, you begin in what the experts call a "cold desert." By the time you reach Kino Bay, in a "hot desert," you will have traversed a marvelous array of climatic and biotic zones. Not a single major desert plant species of the Mexican state of Sonora, for example, grows in the desert of Washington.

Still, from end to end the desert has a particular, severe character about it that sets it apart from other big North American landscapes, and much of this character has to do with the nature of desert rains. Rainfall in most regions of temperate and subtropical deserts is distinguished by four attributes which together set it apart from rain patterns over the rest of the earth.

First, and most obviously, desert precipitation is extraordinarily scanty, but in addition it tends to be episodic (often seasonal), violent, and local. A typical desert rain falls as a short, torrential downpour that will literally flood several square miles of desert but then leave this same ground high and dry for months or even years afterward. Thus, the common desert climatological model is one in which there is so little precipitation that nothing like a thick vegetational ground cover can develop, and this characteristic is accompanied by rare, violent rains which scour and cut the unprotected ground surface.

Among our desert's four main parts—the Chihuahuan, Sonoran, Mojave, and Great Basin—the Chihuahuan provides the most classic example of this climactic phenomenon. Its pronounced "subtropical" rainy season interrupts months and months of dry weather with a few violent storms that come usually in late summer and deliver, depending upon where you are, a total annual precipitation of seven to nine inches. The Mojave has a similar pattern, although its precipitation averages are notably less than those of the Chihuahuan. The Sonoran deviates from this single rainy season characteristic in that much of it has a bimodal rain

Where the desert gives way to northern grasslands: Prairie lupine, wallflower, Indian ricegrass, and bluebunch wheatgrass growing on the edge of the Great Basin Desert. Butte County, Idaho, 1996.

46

pattern: two rainy seasons, during which brief, often violent rains occur, in late summer and again in midwinter.

This picture is a general one, and not as neat as these descriptions imply. For example, one Sonoran Desert locality is known to have gone thirteen years without a drop of rain while others of its regions, including Tucson, Arizona, and its environs, get an average of twelve inches per year. And over large parts of the Mojave, where annual precipitation averages less than two inches, there is, indeed, hardly any rainy season at all.

A brief April rain has watered the dry country, producing an example of perhaps the most spectacular of desert phenomena, the blooming of Mexican gold poppies (*Eschscholtzia mexicana*). Luna County, New Mexico, 1995.

Then there is the Great Basin Desert, whose rains (and snows), as we will see, conform only marginally to the typical pattern. Nevertheless, because of its dryness and occasional torrential storms, in notable respects its desert face reflects much the same desolate quality as those of its three southern neighbors. And this quality, from central Mexico to the British Columbia border, is manifest in the scars left behind by rare tumultuous rains falling on bare desert ground: dry gullies, alluvial fans built outward from the mouths of dry canyons (and composed of rock debris carried down on high water), and ephemeral, often bone-dry, lakes and ponds.

The creation of these scars can take relatively very little time, although they have been in discontinuous process for thousands and millions of years. Hang around the desert for a few months, or a year or two, and you can watch while lakes go dry and floods carve gulches. Additionally, you will see and feel the desert's winds, whose nature is intimately related to its aridity and rains.

Marks of the wind are most noticeable in the way they arrange rock particles over the landscape, producing sand dunes, exposing bedrock, and spreading silt. Silt, finer than sand (and the smallest of rock particles), is the major desert aeolian (wind-borne) product. In the popular mind, deserts connote sand, but ton for ton far more silt than sand is distributed and redistributed by the wind, which picks it up from the rain-scoured desert flats and dry lake beds.

Finally, as regards the severity of the desert's face, there are the marks of the process known as mass wasting. The effects of mass wasting are most dramatic in desertic environments; that is, in regions of little vegetation, heavy rain or snowmelt runoff, sloping ground, and wide variations in air temperature from season to season and often between night and day. The latter of these conditions, extremes of heat and cold, is the initial, essential factor in mass wasting, for it causes the breakdown of bedrock. Searing desert heat in itself is enough to fracture many or most rock types eventually, but wasting is hastened when the temperature swings include freezing. Much of the breaking of exposed desert rock results directly from frost expansion after cracks are invaded first by either condensation or water from rain or snow.

Still, the whole process is agonizingly slow — we are writing in time frames of millions of years. Wasting begins on high slopes and ridge lines, where over the ages exposed bedrock is crumbled not only by heat and cold but by chemical breakdown. Once the rock is broken into transportable pieces, it falls or slides down slope or is carried down by water, until after aeons of time the desert's mountains are flattened out. Travel U.S. 95 from Indian Springs to Beatty, Nevada, and then west on other blacktops across Death Valley to Panamint Springs, California, and you will see mass wasting well on its way. The mountains quite literally stand half buried in their rubble. These, then—ephemeral creeks and ponds, exposed bedrock, rock slides, and wind—and water-swept flats—are the desert's unifying hallmarks.

Generally speaking, these attributes describe all temperate and subtropical deserts, but another characteristic of the North American—its big rivers—is not universally shared. With the exception of the Mojave, which has no proper rivers at all, each of the desert's major parts has its big streams: the Colorado, Columbia, and Rio Grande, to name but three. But while they are fascinating features of the desert, they have very little effect on the biological composition of the dry country lying beyond their floodplains. Heading in exterior mountains, they run entrenched through the desert, and typical desert plants (and animals) range right down to their banks.

And then there are the differences that separate the Chihuahuan, Great Basin, Mojave, and Sonoran. Biologists define the four main parts of the North American Desert (and the rest of the earth's land surfaces, as well) primarily on the differential occurrences of plant species, a scheme of ordering the natural world that had its origins a century ago when C. Hart Merriam conceived of life zones. Merriam, an American working in the western United States, noticed that as you travel from lower to higher latitudes or from lower to higher altitudes you pass through belts, or zones, of different plants or groups of plants.

Particular animal species, or groups of them, often accompany these plants and their communities, but life zones are based mainly on vegetational criteria, as plants more than animals tend to stay put. There are notable exceptions. Among the four subdeserts, the sage grouse is exclusive to the Great Basin, and the bison (a nondesert animal) roamed the Wyoming sagebrush country until the mid-nineteenth century. But on the other hand, such species as the gray wolf, grizzly bear, mule deer, pronghorn antelope, and bighorn sheep ranged over all four subdeserts.

Merriam's North American life zone list contained some half-dozen zones, ranging from "Lower Sonoran" to "Arctic-Alpine." While subsequent refinements have increased this total to eighteen and revised the names of the original zones, even today Merriam's Lower Sonoran and Upper Sonoran (now Southern Desert Scrub and Northern Desert Scrub, respectively) rather accurately describe and encompass all of the desert but for the various desert mountains.

Leaving out the great mountain chains, such as the Sierra Nevada and others that only border the desert, its interior contains numerous ranges and peaks, some of which are very tall. Most Great Basin Desert bedrock is Eocene basalt, forty million years old, that was stretched, thinned, and fractured during the Miocene (five to twenty million years ago) along lines parallel to the Pacific Coast. The resulting narrow mountains—some are one hundred miles long—are lined up in great irregular rows, all pointing north and south but massed from east to west. Many reach elevations of from more than nine thousand feet to more than fourteen thousand feet above sea level. As altitude, as well as latitude, is a life zone determinant, all of Merriam's original zones, including the Arctic–Alpine, occur on a number of these interior desert mountains such as the

Ruby Range in Nevada. These mountains and their accompanying valleys are known as basin-and-range topography, typical of much of the Great Basin Desert.

In addition to life zones, biologists use the concept of *dominant* plants. The Northern Desert Scrub zone, which includes all of the Great Basin Desert, is said to be dominated by two plant genera: *Artemisia,* whose overwhelmingly most common species is big sage; and *Atriplex* (the salt-bushes), whose two principal Great Basin species are fourwing saltbush and shadscale. These three species give the Great Basin Desert its character. Short, robust, and close growing, they express the singular status of this so-called "cold desert."

In addition to its being appreciably larger than the Chihuahuan and Sonoran, and very much larger than the Mojave, the Great Basin Desert contains several distinctive attributes shared only marginally by its southern neighbors. First, and most tellingly, its northern latitudes result in relatively cold winters with air temperatures often reaching zero degrees Fahrenheit or lower, a range that discourages all but the most "cold-adapted" desert plants. Second, Great Basin Desert rains and snows, scanty as they are, typically fall over several months of each year. There are, as we have noted, occasional summer cloudbursts but most precipitation comes in winter. Winter cloud cover is common; solar radiation is slight; evaporation is slow, accordingly; and rainwater and snowmelt, what little there is of them, last over in the ground until summer. Further, Great Basin Desert soils are comparatively rich. Over the past fifteen or twenty thousand years its more northern parts especially have been successively covered with loess (wind-borne glacial silt); alluvial gravels, sands, and silts; volcanic ash; and the humus generated by its native flora.

Thus, because of its soils and climate, including its cold season, while the Great Basin Desert grows relatively few plant species, those well-adapted few grow in abundance.

Big sage, commonly called sagebrush, grows on the best ground, and its individual plants are separated commonly by only two or three yards, while the spaces between and among them often support bunchgrasses. Neither the sage nor the grasses grow densely enough to create a vegetational mat such as the sort found on the shortgrass prairies of northeastern New Mexico that merge with the Chihuahuan Desert. Among the plants of this sagebrush country there are patches of barren ground, but relatively speaking the vegetation here is so thick that some biologists call the northern Great Basin *steppe* rather than desert.

As their collective name implies, the saltbushes are salt tolerant, more so than big sage, and therefore become increasingly abundant, and dominant, as you travel southward through the Great Basin toward its southern border, where the soils are more alkaline and less developed. Roughly south of a line from Cameron, Arizona, to Scotty's Junction, Nevada, you run out of big sage. Further, at about this latitude, the desert

52

This picture of a honey mesquite prairie was taken in May, following nearly fourteen months without a drop of rain. Nevertheless, the mesquite is coming into leaf (the yucca's leaves are green the year around). In wait of rain, annuals may not bloom here for three or four years. Luna County, New Mexico, 1996.

nomenclature, both popular and scholarly, crosses over from English to Spanish. Ephemeral lakes are *playas* (beaches), gulches are *arroyos* (stream or brook). The big, consolidated fans of rock rubble are *bajadas* (slopes) and basins are now *bolsons*, after *bolsos* (bags or purses). The farther south you travel the more intense the sun and warmer the annual temperatures. Soils become poorer and thinner. You reach the Sonoran Desert south of Las Vegas, the Mojave near Scotty's Junction.

With practically no exceptions, big sage does not run southward into either of these two deserts nor into the Chihuahuan, which together with the Mojave and Sonoran is embraced by the Southern Desert Scrub life zone. The saltbushes grow on southward beyond the sagebrush country, but the creosotebush (*Larrea tridentata*) is the single most widespread perennial in all three of the southern deserts, and as such it is designated *dominant* in each of them. It is a modest and spindly plant, on average two or three feet taller than either big sage or the saltbushes, commonly growing to about seven feet. It covers tens of thousands of square miles, over many of which it is the tallest and by far the most noticeable plant.

Because of the heat of the southern deserts and the nature of their soils and rains, the creosote barrens are quite unlike those of the sagebrush. Individual creosotebushes sprout from parent root systems that can be incredibly old, as old as three thousand years or more, and each such parent root may produce dozens of bushes over thousands of square feet of desert floor. Each bush, however, is separated typically by twenty or thirty feet or more of barren ground, whose surface, lacking mulch or loam, consists typically of small gravels. Such barren ground, with or without gravel but whose perennials are widely separated, is what you will find over most of the southern dry country. There are, interestingly enough, some southern desert regions that contain abundant bunchgrasses mixed in with taller plants, but typical surfaces are usually bare of all but scattered perennials.

Here in the south, and again, generally unlike the Great Basin, both plants and animals adapt to what may be called *classic* desert conditions of prolonged aridity. Among vertebrates, to name two of many examples, the Gambel's quail adjusts its nesting season to periods of rain, and the several species of kangaroo rats and mice recycle their urine in order to survive long spans of drought. Among plants, and especially in the absence of winter moisture, seeds of the annuals, such as poppies and verbena, may not germinate for one or several years until a typical, local desert storm brings them to bloom.

But adaptations of the southern desert perennials are the most spectacular. In addition to being spaced out over the ground in order to allocate water, they ward off herbivorous vertebrates by being covered with spines or having unpalatable foliage. And they survive drought, variously, by putting down deep roots in search of moisture, storing water in their tissues (hence the term succulents, whose best-known members are the cacti), having leaves so small that little water is required to support the parent plant, and by producing leaves for brief periods only, following rainstorms.

As dominant as are the creosotebushes, each of the southern deserts has its own distinguishing flora, all of which possess one or more of the above attributes of dryland survival. The Mojave Desert is the smallest and least distinctive of the three southern deserts (although topographically, its dry Death Valley floor, lying 250 feet below sea level, holds the North American record), but the famous Joshua tree, a large yucca, is restricted to the Mojave, as are some highly noticeable cacti.

Purple prickly pear (*Opuntia violacea*) is among the largest of the prickly pears native to the United States; its leaves are the most colorful of all cacti. Pima County, Arizona, 1996.

The Chihuahuan, the next largest after the Great Basin, differs topographically from both the Mojave and the Sonoran in that it is a "high desert." All of it lies from about four thousand to nearly six thousand feet above sea level, and even though it is sunny, dry, and relatively warm, winter temperatures often reach freezing or lower. Chihuahuan Desert flora, therefore, while not cold-adapted to the same degree as Great Basin Desert plants, lack numerous Mojave and Sonoran warm species.

In addition to the dominant creosotebush (which, tellingly, is far too warm-adapted to survive the Great Basin Desert), the signature plants over much of the Chihuahuan, all succulents, are three yuccas, including the tall "soaptree," the agave known as lechuguilla, or Candle of Our Lord; another, the New Mexico agave; and the sotol. These and a few others, among about a thousand endemic plant species, give the Chihuahuan Desert its stamp.

But most grandiose and spectacular of the four subdeserts is the Sonoran. Again, as noted, the creosotebush is dominant, a designation that seems hardly appropriate to most people because of the Sonoran's world-famous giant saguaro cactus. Besides the saguaro there is the nearly as famous organ pipe cactus; the lesser known blue palm and "boojum" of the Sonoran's Baja Peninsula; the southern Sonoran elephant tree; the widespread palo verde; and the southern cardón cactus that is even larger than the saguaro (again, succulents all). The list goes on and on. And to add to all this, the Sonoran runs right down to the sea, so that in addition to a variety of littoral plants which are unique to the Sonoran, it has its equally unique shore fauna, including great sea turtles, to name a single example.

The North American Desert, then, as dry as it is and barren as it seems, is a mosaic of landforms and biomes. In combination, its biological diversities, air temperature ranges, elevations above (and below) sea level, and big, exotic rivers are unmatched among the earth's great deserts. And consequently, the histories of its native tribes reflect a remarkable range of techniques in desert survival.

THE FACE OF THE DESERT

Arroyos result in the first place from the absence of close-growing vegetation combined with violent, episodic rainstorms. But arroyos themselves contribute to further dryness and desiccation by lowering the water table. The deeper an arroyo cuts, the more it drains off subsurface water contained in below-ground saturated soils—the water table.

Forty-five years ago this writer discovered the site of an old Spanish–Mexican town that had been abandoned a century earlier because the bed of the neighboring creek had become so deep, and its flow so scanty, that the settlers could no longer get water to their fields.

The arroyo shown in this picture lies 50 air-miles from the above noted abandoned town. Both of them, and hundreds of others, lie within a large arid region of central New Mexico that is not usually considered part of the true North American Desert. Thus, both reflect the desert's expansion in recent times.

ARROYO

Sandoval County, New Mexico
1991

As uncommon as desert rains are, they are commonly intense. Among the first advice that the would-be desert camper is likely to get is "never pitch your tent in a dry wash." Why? Because in the middle of the night a cloudburst may come roaring down the gully and drown you.

Which brings us to a related characteristic of desert precipitation: Rain, when it comes, tends to be local as well as violent. A few square miles of desert may get a torrential three inches in a single hour, then go without a drop of rain for years afterward. It is hard to exaggerate the grandeur of a desert storm. In an otherwise blue sky it comes as a coal-black curtain full of lightning and thunder and millions of gallons of water. The violence of such a deluge, falling for thirty minutes on an upthrust ridge of fossil dunes, flooded the surrounding desert pictured here.

STORM ON SAN RAFAEL REEF

Emery County, Utah

1986

60

Fᴏʀ ᴀ ʟᴀɴᴅ sᴜʀғᴀᴄᴇ ᴛᴏ ᴀʙsᴏʀʙ ʜᴇᴀᴠʏ ʀᴀɪɴ, it must be covered with absorbent soils and a vegetational mat of one kind or another. But for lack of precipitation, and sustained precipitation particularly, no such mat can grow in a desert where, in addition, soils tend to be hard or otherwise repellent to water. The water from cloudbursts therefore pours down canyons and gullies and runs in sheets over more level ground to the nearest natural gutters, resulting in short-lived but spectacular floods.

Shown here is a late summer storm in a big spread of land called the Red Desert, which is actually the northeasternmost end of the Great Basin Desert. This landscape gets twice the precipitation of most of the Mojave and much of the Sonoran deserts, and it supports a thin cover of grasses as well as small sages and other perennials. But still, these plants are not enough to absorb torrential rains, as witnessed by the scoured slopes of the little hills in the background.

CLOUDBURST ON THE RED DESERT

Fʀᴇᴍᴏɴᴛ Cᴏᴜɴᴛʏ, Wʏᴏᴍɪɴɢ

1989

As you would expect, the southern deserts, the Chihuahuan, Mojave, and Sonoran, have the hottest temperatures. Death Valley, Inyo County, California, holds the Western Hemisphere record of 134 degrees F, but 120-degree readings are common in California, Arizona, Baja California, and Sonora. In these same regions, recorded ground temperatures (as distinct from the in-the-shade air temperatures) have reached a staggering 190 degrees F.

Great Basin Desert temperatures are not as high, but they can be impressive. We remember the summers when some wag would see how many seconds it took to fry an egg on a Yakima sidewalk, and it did not take many. Ground and near-ground summer temperatures create superheated air that covers the desert to a height of hundreds of feet and vaporizes promising summer storms. Hence the virga, or ghost rain, that never reaches the ground.

GHOST RAIN

FREMONT COUNTY, WYOMING
1989

64

THE VOLUME AND ENERGY of a desert rainstorm are awesome. Running over typical barren, hard-surfaced ground, in an hour or two a cloudburst can create arroyos six feet deep from the smallest cracks in the desert floor. Over decades and centuries, these flood channels are deepened and widened by successive storms.

In a flat-country arroyo, the oncoming head of water can be ten feet tall, and in a desert mountain canyon, the waters of a single violent storm, sluicing down from the neighboring slopes, can produce a raging river that will carry twenty-ton boulders hundreds of feet downhill.

The boulders shown in this picture are not of such dimensions. The largest weigh a few hundred pounds, but they lie where they were dropped more than a century ago by the last big flood down this shallow canyon, here in Death Valley, where annual precipitation averages less than two inches.

CANYON FLOOR

INYO COUNTY, CALIFORNIA
1987

66

THERE IS NO SUCH THING as an honest river that rises in a desert, even though a few spring-fed, desert-born rivulets are awarded the title. But there are a fair number of perennial streams, some of them big, that run through one or another part of the North American Desert, and because they have their origins in mountains beyond the desert's boundaries, they are known in the dry country as *exotic* rivers.

The biggest by far are the Columbia and Colorado. In water volume the Rio Grande is sixth or seventh down the line, but it is typically exotic. Note here that it is characteristically entrenched: Its water does not reach into the country on either side, and, accordingly, the desert comes right down to its banks. Therefore, like others of its kind, where it has not been dammed and diverted this celebrated river has little effect on the nature of the surrounding desert landscape.

COSTILLA COUNTY, COLORADO

1989

Nearly every basin has its *playa* ("beach"). Among the rock debris brought down from neighboring high ground by episodic cloudbursts, silt is the finest and lightest and is thus carried the farthest, to the lowermost part of the basin, where it puddles in a shallow lake. Over the centuries, repeated flooding builds a flat clay bed, a playa, on the basin floor.

Some playas hold water every two or three years, others every five or six, and some only once in several decades; it all depends on the vagaries of desert storms. But when playas do fill they can flood a lot of ground. Some such lakes are 10 miles long and a third or half again as wide. All are shallow and ephemeral, however, seldom more than two or three feet deep, and most of them go dry again in less than a year.

PLAYA AND LEAST SANDPIPERS

Punta Kino, Sonora

1989

Both in color and composition this is the most typical of playa floors, characterizing what earth scientists call a dry, or *recharge*, playa. Episodic desert cloudbursts fill these shallow basins with waters that over the following months both evaporate and seep underground. (Recharge refers to this slow, underground flow.) When not covered with water, the playa's floor will most often range in tone or color from a nearly white gray to light yellow. It is composed of fine water-laid and closely wedded silt particles that, after thousands of years of deposition, can result in a floor having a vertical thickness of hundreds of feet. When it is good and dry such a floor is as flat as a tabletop and as solid as a rock, across which, given a big enough playa, you can coax some astonishing speeds from a Chevy pickup.

DRY PLAYA FLOOR

Millard County, Utah
1996

72

Wᴇᴛ, ᴏʀ ᴅɪsᴄʜᴀʀɢᴇ, playas are far less common than so-called dry playas. The latter occur in localities lacking near-surface underground water. Once a dry playa goes dry it leaves behind a bed of solid, hard-packed silt, as shown on page 73. A wet playa, on the other hand, occurs where abundant subsurface water creates seeps, or where, as in this picture, intense prolonged winds have scoured down to the water table. The result is a surface which, while it seems perfectly dry to the innocent traveler, is only the thin crust of a bottomless quagmire.

Drive across one of these sorts of playas, and you will encounter an unforgettable experience. Note in this picture that the rancher has strung his barbed wire to the point of no return, as it were, but all but the most witless of his cattle have long since observed that to venture beyond the end of the fence is to die prematurely.

QUICKSAND

Tᴏʀʀᴀɴᴄᴇ Cᴏᴜɴᴛʏ, Nᴇᴡ Mᴇxɪᴄᴏ
1996

To GEOLOGISTS AND GEOGRAPHERS the North American Desert is not a sandy desert as is, for example, the Sahara. The North American's surfaces consist generally of clays and silts (whose particles are commonly cemented with salt), rock rubble, coarse sands, gravels, and thin loams, none of which lends itself to the creation of dunes. There are exceptions. All four of the subdeserts contain scattered dune localities or colonies that cover at least a few square miles. In the Sonoran Desert of southeasternmost California a continuous string known as the Algodones Dunes is 50 miles long and 5 miles across.

This picture was taken in Death Valley where old Indian dwelling sites are associated rather frequently with its few dune locales. Apparently, Shoshones, Southern Paiutes, and others before them wintered here, building their windbreaks and wickiups in the hollows and hunting a variety of game, from rodents to bighorn sheep.

THE DUNES AT STOVEPIPE WELLS

INYO COUNTY, CALIFORNIA
1986

THE DESERT LITTORAL of Sonora and Baja California once provided food for a dozen or more shore-dwelling tribes. As shown in this picture, on the Sonoran side of the Sea of Cortéz the cardón cactus (*Pachycereus pringlei*) —larger, even, than the saguaro and with equally edible fruit—grows right down to high tide mark. Great forests of cardones occur within a mile or two of the sea. In both regions, scarce drinking water marked the bottom line of survival, but food sources, while not always present in wished for quantity or quality, were by comparison abundant.

Depending upon locality, tide, and season, the littoral and its immediate environs offer cactus fruit, small game, mollusks (including octopuses), turtles, and fishes. On both the Sonoran and Baja shores the desert beaches and headlands are indented by shallow mangrove estuaries, sources of marvelously edible and easily caught or collected oysters, crabs, fishes, birds, and birds' eggs.

WHERE THE DESERT RUNS DOWN TO THE SEA

PUNTA KINO, SONORA

1993

WITHIN THE GENUS *Atriplex* (the saltbushes), none is nearly as pleasing to the aesthetically inclined nature lover as desert holly (*A. hymenelytra*) Except for its size and the color of its leaves—a most elegant light gray—this salt-bush quite closely resembles Christmas holly. Its serrated leaves are remarkably like those of true holly and its fruit looks much like holly berries. Beyond these resemblances, however, Christmas holly and desert holly are about as closely related as ducks and crows.

The former, a big, vigorous bush or tree, requires abundant rain, while desert holly will survive on two or three inches a year. This picture shows both the extraordinarily dry, barren ground in which desert hollies grow and the tough nature of the plant. The young holly has sprouted from the roots of its parent, whose dead limbs testify to one or another desert calamity.

DESERT HOLLY

INYO COUNTY, CALIFORNIA
1987

THIS LANDSCAPE ON THE TEXAS–COAHUILA border is typical not only of much of the Chihuahuan Desert but of desert surfaces found in other parts of the world. The ground is hard-packed, in this instance consisting of clays and small gravels, and dominated by creosotebushes, practically the only plant species able to take hold on this barren floor.

Perennial desert plants characteristically protect themselves from vertebrate herbivores by having spines, thorns, or unpalatable leaves. While the creosotebush has no armor, its foliage is notably toxic to larger animals. On the other hand, like many other plants, creosotebush attracts a variety of invertebrates, including herbivores, that prefer one plant species or genus over all others. One such species—a grasshopper—lives only on creosote leaves.

CHIHUAHUAN DESERT FLOOR

BREWSTER COUNTY, TEXAS
1988

Big sage, by far the dominant plant in the northern Great Basin Desert, requires good ground: ground free of salts, well drained, and well provided with nutrients. But if you start out from the old sagebrush prairies in eastern Washington and travel south through the big sage country of eastern Oregon and northern Nevada you will see the ground becoming gradually but noticeably poorer, more typical of what most desert soils are like: undeveloped, thin, and often salt-saturated.

And south of a line running roughly from Cameron, Arizona, to Scotty's Junction, Nevada, you run out of the Great Basin Desert with its big sage. Meanwhile, however, across this desert's more southern parts, saltbushes (of the genus *Atriplex*), whose species are far more tolerant of poor ground, have become increasingly dominant. Here, in the southeasternmost reach of the Great Basin Desert, fourwing saltbush (*A. canescens*) dominates this salty flat.

SALTBUSH

COSTILLA COUNTY, COLORADO
1988

THE CREOSOTEBUSH (*Larrea tridentata*) is not to be confused with the petroleum-derived creosote used in soaking telephone poles and railroad ties, but after a rain it smells much the same and is the designated dominant plant for all three southern deserts. Indeed, in the Chihuahuan, Mojave, and Sonoran it so noticeably covers and dominates such immense landscapes that its common Mexican name is *gobernador* ("governor").

Travel these southern deserts and you will see thousands of square miles that seem to grow nothing but creosotebushes, typically seven feet tall or better.

CREOSOTEBUSH

SAN BERNARDINO COUNTY, CALIFORNIA

1994

TYPICAL DESERT PLAYAS are so salt-impregnated that they support few, if any, plants, and even beyond the playas' margins, desert valley floors are often vegetated with species adapted to relatively salty ground and hard-packed clayey soils. This is true especially of the desert's southern parts, where most of its celebrated array of dryland plants are not to be found out in the flat country.

To the contrary, if you are looking for the famous "cactus gardens" of the southern desert look on the high ground—the rocky slopes and canyon sides—where the broken surface is aerated, the salts have been washed downhill, and thin as the soil may be the decaying rock itself provides certain nutrients. Here, accompanied by ocotillos and palo verdes, note the abundant teddy bear chollas and the young saguaros. More than a dozen other cactus species grow on the ridges in the background.

HIGH GROUND

YUMA COUNTY, ARIZONA
1989

THE GENUS *Opuntia* has more species than all other cactus genera put together. Its more than fifty North American kinds are of two distinctive types: the chollas and the prickly pears. Chollas, despite their being more or less attractive, bear incredible numbers of irritating spines and fruit that is unfit for humans. In this traveler's opinion, unless you are a botanist, cactus wren, or peccary, a cholla has few redeeming qualities.

Prickly pears are different. Their spines are not nearly as obnoxious as the chollas', and most of them produce delectable, nutritious fruit high in vitamin C and calcium, from which the desert peoples derived notable sustenance through the ages. Some of the big southern desert prickly pears bear fruit two inches long; others, as with those of this little northernmost species (*O. erinacea*), are as big as thimbles.

A NORTH COUNTRY PRICKLY PEAR

YAKIMA COUNTY, WASHINGTON

1989

90

IN SOUTHWESTERNMOST NEW MEXICO you look for agaves (*Agave* sp.) mainly in the rocky hills and little canyons west of Lordsburg and south of Interstate 10, and there are a few in the breaks of the Gila River on the Arizona border. This country is separated from the wooded Mogollon Mountains to the north and east by playas and big desert flats of dense clay soils or other fine stuff in which agaves will not grow.

Still, there are some agave colonies of both natural and human distribution on the flanks of the Mogollons, among live oaks, junipers, and ponderosa pines—miles beyond the Chihuahuan Desert proper and miles beyond the agaves' principal range. This picture of one of these colonies shows a cluster of a few dozen plants whose progenitors' seeds or sprouts were most probably carried here centuries ago by Indians who wanted this excellent vegetable handy to their seasonal upland encampments. Note the several stages of maturity.

THE OCOTILLO (*Fouquieria splendens*) is native to the Chihuahuan, Mojave, and Sonoran deserts, and no dryland plant is more elegant. Commonly it has twenty or thirty or more stalks, ten to fifteen feet long, from the tips of which in a good year bloom brilliant red flower clusters. Its aesthetic ranking among the old-time desert people is not a matter of record, but the ocotillo was and still is of remarkable utilitarian value.

Ocotillo thorns, as much as an inch long, are needle sharp and line each stalk from base to tip. The stalks will take root if cut off in, say, seven-foot lengths, stuck in the ground, and given a little water. A few hundred stalks, planted in a tight row, make the most formidable house-hold fence you can imagine. Shorn of their thorns, lashed end to end, and bent into hoops, the tough, flexible stalks have served as house frames for uncounted centuries.

OCOTILLO

LAGUNA DE LA CRUZ, SONORA
1989

94

THE CALIFORNIA FAN PALM (*Washingtonia filifera*) is now a favorite ornamental tree in much of the Southwest, but it was restricted prehistorically to scattered groves in the Mojave and Sonoran deserts, where its trees marked the locations of widely scattered springs. Commonly, it was a long day's walk—or more—from one spring to another, but in addition to their essential water the palm oases provided the desert people with housing, clothing, utensils, and food.

As the raw materials of manufacture, palm fronds were made into sandals, burden baskets, hats, and roofing, and other parts of the tree were fashioned into house posts, beams, and cooking ware. As food, blossoms were eaten raw, and the tiny fruit and its seeds were pounded and ground into flour. And camping some distance away and downwind from the springs themselves, native hunters ambushed mule deer and bighorns coming down to drink.

CALIFORNIA FAN PALM

CATAVIÑA OASIS, BAJA CALIFORNIA NORTE

1988

IN THE OLD DAYS, before the introductions of horses, cattle, and domestic sheep, parts of the Chihuahuan and Sonoran deserts contained abundant grasses but relatively few of the more usual desert plants. Some of these grassy regions survive still. This is not to say that they are grasslands in the common sense of the term, as applied, for example, to the shortgrass and long grass prairies east of the Rockies.

For one thing, like Great Basin Desert grasses, the Chihuahuan and Sonoran species do not generate the dense sod mats characteristic of true grasslands, and for another, these southern dry-country grasses are adapted to hard, somewhat salty soil. Here, on the broad Chihuahuan Desert floors of southwestern New Mexico, clumps of grasses of several species are separated typically by bare, unvegetated ground. And except for the associated soaptree yuccas, succulents and others of the usual Chihuahuan Desert assemblage are scarce.

THE BIG FLATS

HIDALGO COUNTY, NEW MEXICO
1989

98

THE TAMARISK (*Tamarix chinensis*), or salt-cedar, native to the dry country bordering the Mediterranean, is abundant in the interior American West, but just how and when it got here remain a mystery. Depending upon which expert you ask, it came with the Spanish conquistadors of the sixteenth and seventeenth centuries or with an American tourist three hundred years later. And there are other explanations.

In any event, as pretty a shrub as it is, great thickets of tamarisk have taken over thousands of square miles of the North American Desert. It grows mainly along the banks and in the floodplains of both perennial and intermittent desert streams—arroyos and the like. Its trunks make indifferent fence posts and reasonably adequate firewood, but against these modest virtues there are its long roots and insatiable thirst. Where it can, it will suck the desert dry. In other words, the tamarisk is a pest.

TAMARISK

OTERO COUNTY, NEW MEXICO
1986

100

QUITE PROBABLY, the mourning dove (*Zenaida macroura*) is the most common of all of the desert's birds. And unlike most of them, such as the celebrated roadrunner, mourning doves range to every corner of the desert, as well as far beyond its boundaries, where in season they can occur in concentrations of thousands. In March, drive the 60 miles from Bahía de Kino to Hermosillo (the capital of Sonora), and clouds and legions of them will fly up ahead of your car.

Mourning doves are hardly bigger than robbins. They lay two pure white eggs in flimsy nests in any bush or tall cactus available or even on the ground. Every predatory reptile, bird, and desert mammal eats mourning doves and their eggs. Still, they survive by the millions, subsisting largely on the seeds of desert plants. Here, two of these foragers have left their tracks on a dune overlooking the Sea of Cortéz.

DOVE TRACKS

BAHÍA DE KINO, SONORA
1986

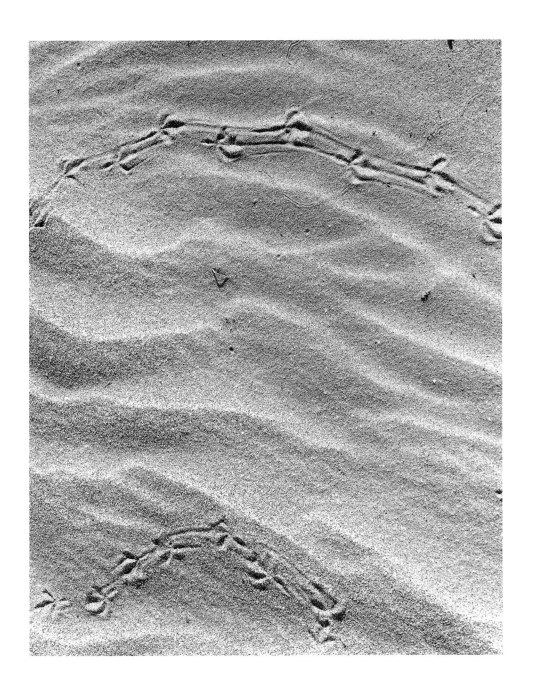

ANTS ARE AMONG the most ubiquitous of the desert's small creatures. In fact, they are so numerous that over large parts of the northern big sage grazing lands their biomass rather astonishingly exceeds that of domestic cattle. And though they are disliked by desert-dwelling humans, and especially by modern-day campers, they are important in the desert's scheme of things. Their burrowings aerate and mulch the soil, and some of them distribute and "sow," as it were, the seeds of dry-country plants.

This diminutive pyramid, four inches tall and eight inches in diameter, was built by so-called leaf cutters, ants whose two genera belong mainly to tropical America and whose northernmost desert colonies reach Arizona and Texas. The adults of this species (*Acromyrmex versicolor*) cut green leaves from neighboring plants, chew them into a special gruel, and spread the mixture on the floors of subterranean galleries. There, it produces a particular fungus, the essential food for the leaf cutters' young.

LEAF CUTTERS' PYRAMID

SERI COAST, SONORA
1990

104

An adult cliff swallow (*Hirúndo pyrrhonóta*) weighs one and a half ounces, hunts on the wing from dawn until dark, and requires daily one-fourth of its weight in insect food. Finding food is hardly a problem; the desert contains enormous numbers of insects. Nor are cliff swallows beset by predators. Agile hawks take only a few of them, and their nests are out of reach to all but the most enterprising bull snake or weasel.

The problem is finding mud with which to build their adobe houses. Because in the desert mud can be hard to come by, this is the major limiting factor in where they establish their colonies. And while you are more a poet than a scientist if you suggest that the ancient Anasazi and other early southwestern cliff dwellers got the idea from swallows, who can tell? The swallows were here first.

SWALLOWS' NESTS

VALENCIA COUNTY, NEW MEXICO
1990

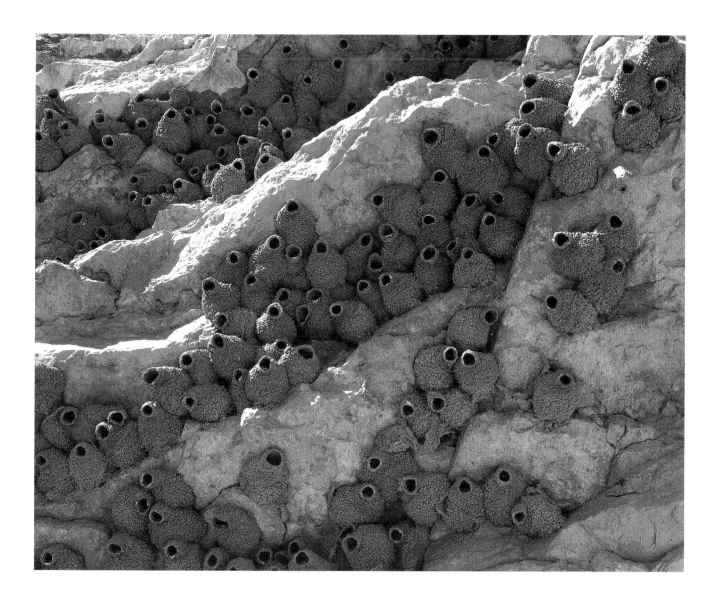

Produced in small pods reminiscent of those of domestic beans, the seeds of the honey mesquite (*Prosopis glandulosa*) were notable fare among native tribes of the desert's southern parts. Stone-ground into meal and served up as gruel or porridge, they provided the main source of wild-plant protein. Not a succulent, the thorny, ligneous parent plant can reach heights of twenty-five feet or more. Its hard, close-grained wood has served equally well in the manufacture of ancient weaponry and modern gun stocks.

The tree tolerates a wide range of desert environmental niches or locales, ranging from rocky ground to clay flats to dunes. It is distinguished further by the length of its root system, which in search of water has been traced to a phenomenal sixty vertical feet below ground surface. Thus, among such foragers as the Southern Paiutes, it provided food in even the driest parts of the desert.

HONEY MESQUITE

Inyo County, California
1986

WHILE TO ECOLOGISTS the creosotebush dominates the Sonoran Desert, the saguaro (*Carnegiea gigantea*) is its popular hallmark, and north of the Mexican border it is by far the largest cactus. A big one is taller than fifty feet, may weigh more than five tons, and may be two hundred years old. Like many cacti, saguaros prefer rocky, usually sloping ground, and often precipitous mountainsides.

For the native tribes of the Arizona–Sonoran borderlands, saguaro fruit—two and a half to three inches long—was probably the most dependable of all food sources and among the most nutritious. Its seeds were ground into a sort of butter, the pulp was eaten raw or cooked, and its fermented juice was used as a personality adjuster. Tohono Oód (Papago) Indian economy was so affiliated with saguaro fruit that these desert people designated the late June harvest season as the beginning of the new year.

SAGUAROS

COCHISE COUNTY, ARIZONA
1986

Desert lore has it that the Joshua tree (*Yucca brevifolia*) was named in 1851 by the Mormon leader Elisha Hunt who, while crossing the Mojave Desert, turned to his followers and said, "Look brethren . . . these green trees are lifting their arms to heaven in supplication. We shall call them Joshua trees!"

In any case, this largest of the yuccas nearly exclusively belongs to the Mojave, and because of its size (some are more than thirty-five feet tall) it is unmistakable. Further, and most remarkable to this traveler, is that Joshua trees occur commonly as forests, thousands of them covering many square miles of exceptionally dry landscapes.

Although far more abundant than the Mojave's California fan palm, which requires surface water, this big yucca played a parallel role in aboriginal native economy. Its buds and seeds were eaten, and among other artifacts its fibers and roots provided for baskets, sandals, carrying nets, dyes, and shampoos.

JOSHUA TREES

RIVERSIDE COUNTY, CALIFORNIA
1987

112

Considering all of the desert's regions, yuccas are even more noticeable than cacti, even though the latter comprise several genera and dozens and dozens of species. The yuccas, succulents whose few species belong to the genus *Yucca*, vary in size from the little, Great Plains form, about four feet tall, to the Joshua tree, sometimes taller than thirty-five feet.

Considering that this is principally an arid-lands genus, its species tolerate wide latitudinal and altitudinal ranges. To name one example, the above-noted Great Plains yucca—known to cowboys as Spanish bayonet—grows from the Texas Panhandle clear to the prairies of Alberta, Canada. Depending upon the species, the young stalks, flower buds, fruit, and seeds were eaten among aboriginal tribes, and the spiny leaves were used in the manufacture of sandals, baskets, and other artifacts. In the case of the species pictured here (*Y. elata*), soap was made from the roots.

SOAPTREE YUCCA

Doña Ana County, New Mexico
1987

SOUTH OF THE U.S. BORDER, the southwesternmost part of the desert contains scattered oases of both the California fan palm and the Mexican blue palm (*Sabal uresana*), the two being so similar looking that it taxes the casual nature lover to tell the difference. Here, at the oasis of Cataviña, the two species are scattered along a few miles of sandy arroyo which in places holds pools and trickles of perennial water, without which there would be no oasis.

The Indians here were Cochimi, closely related to those by the same name living farther south and one of about twelve Baja tribes all of whom, because of the narrowness of the peninsula, had access to the resources of both desert and sea.

Cultural symbols and visual
communication, petroglyphs
chart the course of Native
America. The figures shown
here depict the impact of the
Spanish upon the Indian way
of life. San Juan County, Utah,
1996.

WHEN CORONADO REACHED THE RIO GRANDE in 1540, the desert was occupied by some sixty native tribes of various languages and technologies. Every square mile of the desert lay within the boundaries of one or another tribal territory, even though there were, and are, tens of thousands of square miles which would seem to defy human colonization. Drive any of several possible routes generally southward from Las Vegas, Nevada, to Twentynine Palms, California, and you will wonder how aboriginal people could ever have survived such a totally stark wilderness. But survive they did, as we shall explain, and handily at that.

Less amenable to explanation is the question of why and how native tribes became desert people in the first place. We would venture that most of them arrived originally either because they were crowded into the desert by other more aggressive or numerically powerful tribes or that they came during more salubrious times (toward the end of the Wisconsin Glacial Stage, for example) and over the millennia adapted to arid-land life as the desert evolved. But be that as it may, those barren landscapes between Las

Vegas and Twentynine Palms reflect only one of the desert's several principal environments which, as austere and demanding as all of them are, supported a remarkable spectrum of human economies.

Aboriginally, less than 10 percent of the desert's total land area was inhabited by tribes who possessed domestic food plants or animals. (Except for the dog, and the problematical exception of the wild turkey, no North American tribe had domestic animals.) Rather, most all of the dry country was claimed by foragers who variously were hunters, fishers, and gatherers. Most such tribes were split into several bands, communities of a few families, and because wild food resources were so thinly distributed, each band required an impressively large territory, sometimes a thousand square miles or more. Accordingly, population densities were low, often as low as or lower than one person per 40 or 50 square miles.

With few exceptions, plants rather than animals appear to have been the principal food source throughout all of the desert, certainly in variety and quantity, if not always in nutritional value. Large animals were especially hard to come by. Except for the Eastern Shoshones, who hunted bison in the Great Basin Desert's northeasternmost corner (the so-called "Red Desert" of Wyoming), no desert tribe based any major part of its

Desert-dwelling people have long used prickly pear cacti (*Opuntia* sp.) as a food source. The pads and fruits (tunas) are edible, the latter being sweet in flavor. Pima County, Arizona, 1996.

subsistence economy on big-game hunting. Mule deer, pronghorns, and bighorn sheep occurred across nearly all of the desert, and in parts of the Chihuahuan and Sonoran there were the small Coues' or "Sonoran" white-tailed deer and the small collared peccary (*javelina*). But as important, in theory, as these animals seem to have been, they were so scattered, and often so scarce, that the killing of a fat mule deer buck or bighorn ram was cause for celebration.

Far more common in the diets of the desert people were the smaller creatures. "Rabbit drives," in which these animals were herded into nets or killed with sticks and clubs, were practiced from one end of the desert to the other. Fifteen or more species of other rodents were eaten. Several birds were of value, including, discontinuously across the dry country, waterfowl, the wild turkey, and grouse and quail. In some regions, even insects were important fare. But again, with few exceptions plants were the mainstay.

Generally speaking, the smallest aboriginal populations and lowest population densities occurred in the Great Basin Desert (especially the immense basin from which it gets its name) and in neighboring parts of the Mojave. Tens of thousands of square miles of dry landscapes such as those lying across Utah and Nevada west of Salt Lake City were as barren as any North American human environment, not excepting the Arctic. This hostile countryside was occupied by Gosiutes, Northern Paiutes, Western Shoshones, and others who survived by eating literally anything that provided sustenance. Wild edible plant species ranged from grasses to cattails to piñon pine nuts on the flanks of isolated ranges, but the typical band territory, consisting largely of salt flats and sagebrush–saltbush prairies, supported a relatively narrow range of food plants.

Without animal fat and protein the people would have starved, or at the very least suffered from dietary disease, although, as noted, food ani-

121

mals were generally scarcer than plants. The most sought after were the above-noted big game. Rabbits and hares were far more common. Where there was water there were sometimes waterfowl, and in rare scattered parts of the basin proper there were fishes. But for some bands, all of these vertebrates put together were not enough. In search of animal protein even insects became significant. Each year various bands herded millions of grasshoppers into semisubterranean traps, and harvesting the larvae of a certain fly, again by the millions, was another typical endeavor.

In addition to the buffalo available to the Eastern Shoshones, the tribes of central Washington and its environs were offered another exception to these bleak realities of the Great Basin Desert. Its northwestern-most reaches, the dry big-sage country of Washington, Oregon, and Idaho are cut by the exotic Columbia River and its tributaries, which harbored a remarkable bounty of freshwater resources. Salmon by the millions annually ascended these desert streams, and together with trout of three species there were squawfish, mountain whitefish, white sturgeon to astonishing lengths of thirteen feet, and shoals of freshwater mussels.

These abundances contributed to the quite comfortable lives of such sagebrush tribes as the Yakimas, whose economies were enhanced further by seasonal exploitations of forest and high-mountain food sources. (We remember well, before the wholesale damming of the Columbia, the ruins of substantial prehistoric villages, with their semisubterranean houses and deep kitchen dumps of mussel shells, that lined the river's banks upriver and down from the Wanapum encampment spoken of in the preface to this book.) Still, overall, survival in the Great Basin Desert put the acid test to human ingenuity.

Subsistence sources were easier to come by in the three southern subdeserts. As described in the preceding essay, the Sonoran particularly, because of its latitude and bimodal rain pattern, produces an exceptional variety of plants. In addition to other cacti, the Sonoran contains the big organ pipe, the giant saguaro, and the even larger cardón, the fruits of all three of which are large, abundant in season, and nourishing. The Chihuahuan and the Mojave lack these three big species, but both they and the Sonoran have numerous other edible cacti, added to several species of agaves and yuccas, and the mesquites, whose beans were a primary staple among all southern tribes. In addition to these plants were the sorts of vertebrates we have listed.

There were a few informative variations on this general picture of Chihuahuan, Mojave, and Sonoran foraging. Referring back to those grim landscapes of the Mojave lying southward from Las Vegas, the Serrano Indians, of the general region of Twentynine Palms, augmented typical southern foragers' fare with the seeds and fruit of native palms, which grow at widely scattered oases and were so valued that they were tended and curated almost as if they were domestic trees.

But perhaps the most remarkable foraging economies in all of the desert were those of the Seri and their neighbors, who lived—as do their few descendants—on the coasts of the Sea of Cortéz. Most of the Seri country lay north of Bahía de Kino, a shallow, windswept embayment on the mainland shore of the Mexican state of Sonora, and included a broad coastal strip and neighboring islands. Take the dirt truck road northward from Kino and you will traverse the most elegant stretch of desert in North America, and nearly the driest and hottest.

Close eastward stands a string of sharp desert hills, the Sierra Seri. On your left, over gray, igneous gravel, the desert runs down to high tide mark. But there is no water here except for the sea. Unless you arrive after a rare winter rain, or know the locations of scarce hidden springs, you can die of thirst here.

Plants, as usual, loomed large in the Seri diet. About seventy-five species were eaten, most of them small and many of them grains, including the seeds of the marine eel grass. And nearly all of the food plants, including the abundant mesquite, saguaro, cardón, and organ pipe, grow either down to the beaches or to within 2 or 3 miles of salt water. The ubiquitous mule deer, pronghorn, and bighorn were more or less similarly available, as were the peccary and the usual roster of lesser terrestrial vertebrates.

Pictographs of red ocher (iron hematite) survive beside the ruins of a Mogollon village occupied from about A.D. 1277 to 1300. Grant County, New Mexico, 1996.

But this was only the half of it. The sea, including its estuaries, provided, and does still, a seemingly endless list of food animals, from ninety-foot stranded whales to mangrove oysters. (Armed only with a pocket knife, at low tide you can wander down a Seri estuary eating oysters on the half shell.) To date, for example, some three hundred species of crabs alone (not all of them practically available or edible) have been identified from the Sea of Cortéz, and the search for new species continues. There are sea turtles that weigh hundreds of pounds, thousands of wintering brant geese, and many times that number of redhead ducks.

The Seri built frail-looking little reed boats that turned out to be better among the straits and islands than the Spanish galleons. They made big water storage vessels of pottery so fine and thin that the type is known to archaeologists as Seri Eggshell. And they wore winter suits of brown pelican skins, feathers attached.

Still, from the poorest to the most well-to-do, survival among the desert foragers demanded an annual round of traveling from one place to the next. Probably, the Yakimas and their neighbors came as close as any of these tribes to a sedentary or settled way of life. Their riverine villages were large (sometimes two hundred people or more), and among other, more temporary dwellings they lived in the "permanent" semisubterranean houses mentioned earlier. Yet even the Yakimas spent parts of each year foraging in the uplands and elsewhere beyond the big river valleys. And for practically all of the rest, including the Seri and the few other shore-dwelling tribes of western Sonora and Baja California, their lives consisted typically of moving five or seven or more times a year from one important place to the next, carrying their possessions on their backs and living in houses easy to build and just as easy to abandon.

But then there were the desert farmers. By the time of Christ, corn, beans, and squash had reached present-day Arizona from the Valley of Mexico; they have been cultivated ever since by several dozen western tribes. The hows and whys of the introductions of these three domestic food plants remain unknown. Possibly, they were carried northward from far down in Mexico by immigrants who came as settlers to the American Southwest. More probably, their seeds and their techniques of cultivation were passed along ancient trade routes from one new farming locality to the next, to be adopted eventually by various foraging peoples living in or near the desert.

For most of these people, farming was to remain as an adjunct only, and often a minor adjunct at that, to hunting, fishing, and gathering, but for others it resulted in civilization. When Coronado's troops found Hopi Pueblo in 1540, its cluster of close-lying villages contained an estimated eight thousand people. Hopi, Zuni, and several other southwestern farming communities (which survive vigorously to this day) were built, as it were, quite exclusively on corn, beans, and squash. (For what it is worth, with a population of eight thousand, Hopi was larger than 95 percent of modern U.S. farming towns.)

When the Spaniards first arrived, these big Pueblo Indian towns of Arizona and New Mexico had long since developed complex religious, social, and political systems. There were organized work forces, construction and field bosses, and a hierarchy of more lofty ranks including priests and prophets. And there were far-flung networks of trade and communication. The Hopi, for example, made regular, perhaps annual, journeys to the Sea of Cortéz, a round-trip of some 700 *air* miles, not to be equated with *walking* miles.

All these accomplishments—and many more—stemmed from farming those humble vegetables: corn, beans, and squash. The usual list of desert food vertebrates was eaten, and quite probably their dietary values were critically important. But the marvelously successful productions of these three domestic plants with sophisticated dryland techniques of soil fertilization and irrigation, and the resulting accumulations of crop surpluses, were the key to Pueblo civilization, all the more remarkable because of the total absence of wheeled vehicles, metal tools, or beasts of burden.

Before the coming of the Spaniards, these big societies, including the Hopi, were what archaeologists call collectively the Anasazi. By A.D. 900, or thereabouts, three tribal aggregates whose territories lay mainly north of the U.S.–Mexican boundary and included, collectively, parts of the Chihuahuan, Great Basin, and Sonoran deserts had established farming communities of hundreds and sometimes thousands of inhabitants. These three traditions are known to prehistorians as the Anasazi, Hohokam, and Mogollon cultures, the latter two of which somewhat mysteriously passed out of the picture centuries before the earliest Spanish explorations. But the Anasazi survived to become today's modern Pueblos of the Rio Grande Valley, western New Mexico, and eastern Arizona, many at the sites of their prehistoric towns.

Probably none of the ancient Anasazi farming centers had populations as large as those of Hopi at the time of European contact, but certain Anasazi achievements, most spectacularly their architecture, have over the past century both delighted and confounded archaeologists. First among these monumental ruins are those of Chaco Canyon in northwestern New Mexico.

Chaco Canyon lies squarely in a Great Basin Desert environment. It is surrounded by several thousand square miles of big sage and saltbushes, a landscape that has changed very little, if at all, since well before about A.D. 850, the inaugural years of three centuries of Chacoan grandeur. So it is uncertain as to just why the splendors of Chaco developed here in the first place, especially since the setting deviates noticeably from the less desertic locales of the other big Anasazi settlements.

Wrought-iron latch on the main doors of the Franciscan Mission San Xavier del Bac, Tohono Oód (Papago) Reservation. Pima County, Arizona, 1996.

But in any event, by means of complex water-control systems, the Chacoans conserved what rain the desert storms gave them, irrigated their corn, beans, and squash, and built a metropolis. Over that three-hundred-year span, and particularly during the "Classic Bonito" phase of A.D. 1020 to 1120, they constructed an estimated 200 to 400 miles of carefully graded roads (honest roads, not footpaths), and in addition to hundreds of vernacular dwellings in 10 linear miles of canyon built fifteen awe-inspiring towns of mortared stone, the likes of which the Anasazi world had never seen. They established colonies (outliers) that extended throughout the Four Corners region (where Arizona, Utah, Colorado, and New Mexico join), made the finest of prehistoric North American pottery, and trafficked in large quantities of turquoise, jet, and parrot feathers. The list goes on and on.

And then, for reasons unknown in their entireties, in about A.D. 1150 the whole grand enterprise was abandoned and Chaco fell to ruin. Explanations for the rise and fall of Chaco, as well as for the origins and fortunes of others of the desert tribes, have yet to meet enthusiastic agreement among modern scholars. But the fact remains that from the grasshopper eaters to the corn growers, survival in the desert testifies to unique resources and resourcefulness both.

THE DESERT PEOPLE

For two thousand years the Seri Indians have camped on the Sonoran shore of the Sea of Cortéz in one of the most dry and forbidding parts of North America. The desert runs right down to high-tide mark, and potable water is the most precious of commodities. Still, the Seri are among those desert foragers who lived quite well.

They hunted land animals, but their diet consisted overwhelmingly of terrestrial plants and the bounty of the sea. As shown by this deserted camp, their traditional dwellings are made of the long, nodding stems of ocotillos, cut off at ground level, stripped of their thorns, and tied together in hoops to form hemispherical frames. Covered with brush or scraps of canvas they are good houses, windproof, roomy to a point, and easily made. Note in the foreground the tracks of that ultimate desert survivalist, the coyote, inquiring here of any scraps left behind.

A TURTLE HUNTERS' CAMP

The Seri Coast, Sonora
1988

130

Among foraging tribes—hunting, fishing, gathering peoples—it is axiomatic that in order to survive they travel from season to season in search of food sources, sources which according to time of year are available variously in one or another locality. These necessary rounds tend to discourage both permanent dwellings and other artifacts which are not easily carried or cannot be made on the spot or which, as in the case of heavy milling stones, cannot be left behind at seed-harvesting places to be used again the following year.

All this results in an austere inventory of worldly possessions, but an inventory that among its other items universally contains artifacts of play and adornment. For example, among the Seri, tiny, fired-clay human figurines were the most common of children's toys. And these olive shell beads, their string long since rotted away, are another example.

SERI BEADS

Bahía de Kino, Sonora
1986

132

Here is a desert in which drinking water was so scarce that along the Seri's mainland coast—more than 200 air miles—there were just eight permanent springs. But for a desert, food was plentiful. As an anthropologist who has seen a lot of archaeological sites, none has impressed this writer more than the middens—the garbage dumps—that, lying back of the beaches, line the Seri coast from end to end.

These middens, some of them dating back many centuries, contain the shells and bones of millions of bivalves, sea snails, crabs, fishes, turtles, pelicans, dolphins, whales, and seals. There are great piles of pen shells, the very large, fragile bivalves that grow upright in shallow water, and heaps of oysters and the lovely, big murex snails (*Murex nigritis*). This picture shows the Seri way of getting at the animal, a culinary treat.

BLACK MUREX

Bahía de Kino, Sonora
1988

At another time in history, salmon of five species in numbers well into the fifteen millions annually ascended the Columbia River to spawn and die in its tributaries. Once into the sagebrush country, beyond where the Columbia cuts through the Cascade Mountains to the sea, the salmon were intercepted by native fishermen at narrows and falls in the big desert rivers. Perched on a flimsy platform of stone-hewn planks slung to the side of a cliff, the fisherman dipped his long-handled net when a salmon appeared in the foam below.

Given that a big chinook salmon often weighed seventy pounds or more, you may appreciate that tying into one of those monsters was a sporting proposition. Civilization has killed off most of the salmon, and most modern-day Indians have given up this ancient technique, but at certain narrows a few native fishermen take their chances still.

SALMON FISHER'S ROOST

Wasco County, Oregon
1994

While between them big sage (*Artemisia tridentata*) and creosote-bush (*Larrea tridentata*) dominate the North American Desert, neither is good to eat. Curiously, given the armored characteristics of so many desert plants (including the most important edible ones), both of these plants lack spines or thorns. The creosotebush hardly needs them; its foliage is toxic to vertebrate herbivores. Sagebrush is not so protected. Deer, sage grouse, and others browse its leaves, but it offers nothing in the way of human food.

On the other hand, both plants were known among the desert people for their curative values, and among we moderns they are included in various practices of medicine. Among Great Basin Desert tribes, sweet-smelling big sage smoke was essential to the purifying sweat bath. And from there across the northern desert sagebrush teas and ointments cured a whole range of intestinal ailments, skin infections, and aches of muscle, joint, and bone.

NATIVE MEDICINE

Harney County, Oregon
1996

138

In present-day New Mexico, corn was cultivated as early as 1500 B.C., and by A.D. 1000 both there and in other parts of the American Southwest, desert and semidesert farming had resulted in prosperous sedentation. The crops were corn, beans, and squash, which had been introduced at various times from Mexico and which were irrigated by the desert farming tribes from check dams built in perennial or intermittent streams or by rainwater storage and conservation systems.

Among those prehistoric farming tribes, the Mogollon people settled across southern New Mexico and adjacent regions, planting both in wooded upland valleys and in creosote desert, including such unlikely places as the Tularosa Basin, the most desolate stretch of Chihuahuan Desert in all of New Mexico. This portrait overlooks traces of long-abandoned farm plots (A.D. 900–1200) along a little creek on the eastern edge of the Tularosa Basin.

MOGOLLON PETROGLYPH

OTERO COUNTY, NEW MEXICO
1990

140

PLANTS, WHETHER WILD OR DOMESTICATED, were not enough to sustain desert people; they craved animal protein and fat as well. Skeletons of the desert farmers, especially, show diseases resulting from inadequate animal protein. Sought-after animals ranged from invertebrates to big game. Among the latter, the mule deer, pronghorn, and bighorn sheep occurred in limited numbers in most of the desert and, because of their size and seasonal fatness, were hunted with what may be imagined was often a sort of desperate enthusiasm.

The pronghorn (*Antilocapra americana*) shown here was painted by an artist of the Mogollon Culture (A.D. 200–1350), whose people cultivated corn, beans, and squash in and near the Chihuahuan Desert of southern New Mexico.

GRANT COUNTY, NEW MEXICO
1995

Even before the coming of white men and their firearms, the desert contained relatively few bighorns (*Ovis canadensis*). Among thousands of excavated archaeological sites, their bones are scarce. But curiously, and possibly because this wild sheep was of religious as well as economic significance, it is depicted commonly in prehistoric rock art from one end of the desert to the other. This petroglyph, with its shamanistic figure at top center, tells of an event or a wished-for event in the lives of the so-called Fremont people, Indians who farmed the sagebrush canyons of east-central Utah from A.D. 600 to 1300. Possibly the panorama commemorates an extraordinarily successful bighorn slaughter—a summer hunt in which about thirty-five ewes and lambs (no adult rams are shown) were surrounded and killed. On the other hand, it may denote hunters' magic, an imitation of a hunt fervently wished for.

144

F<small>EW, IF ANY,</small> of the desert's ancient artifacts are more intriguing than this one, which combines art, detailed knowledge of natural history, and perhaps sophisticated culinary taste. Two thousand years old and made of woven reeds, the decoy shown here, and twelve others like it, was recovered from Lovelock Cave in northwestern Nevada. This is, and was, barren sagebrush–saltbush country, relieved only by a few alkali ponds. To survive here, the desert people ate practically any edible plant or animal they could lay their hands on, including various ducks and geese that stopped over on their way to and from more salubrious environments.

But this decoy does not imitate just any old duck. The treatment of its head and bill identifies it unmistakably as a canvasback (*Aythya valisineria*), which makes you wonder, because from colonial times onward, gourmets have ranked the canvasback first among all North American waterfowl.

THE NAVAJOS, and their close relatives the Apaches, have lived in the desert for at least six centuries, and perhaps for much longer. Their native languages are Athapaskan, a linguistic stock whose speakers with few exceptions dwell in the forests of western Canada and Alaska, from which regions the Navajos and Apaches immigrated southward.

Among the most fascinating elements of traditional Navajo material culture is their old-time dwelling, the hogan. It is hexagonal in plan, roofed with beams and smaller members, and covered with dirt. Except for the absence of a sunken floor and entrance passage, the hogan's design is that of an ages-old northland house, a house of a kind—in both northern Eurasia and northern North America—built to withstand bitter cold.

In the desert Southwest, the subterranean floor and entryway have long since been discarded as unnecessary.

HOGAN

NAVAJO COUNTY, ARIZONA
1995

NORTH OF THE KINGDOMS of the Toltecs and Aztecs, Pueblo Bonito remains the star in the crown of prehistoric North American architecture. Largest of the fifteen major Chaco Canyon "towns," its earliest walls were laid about A.D. 850, and the last of its additions and improvements were completed three hundred years later. By A.D. 1100 Pueblo Bonito was four stories tall, had six hundred rooms, and encompassed a great, elevated plaza containing more than forty kivas (subterranean ceremonial structures).

To modern archaeologists, architects, and stonemasons, as well as to the rest of us, its splendor is well nigh overwhelming, and therein lies an intriguing question. Archaeologists, including some of the very best, have dug at Pueblo Bonito for a hundred years. But to this day, scholars disagree on its purpose. Was it a great apartment house, a temple, a trade center, a political edifice? We may never know.

PUEBLO BONITO: SOUTHEAST ELEVATION

SAN JUAN COUNTY, NEW MEXICO
1995

150

ARCHAEOLOGICAL EVIDENCE shows clearly that in prehistoric times both cultural and environmental events influenced profoundly the lives of various desert tribes. Among other such events, the evolution of the desert's climates, native warfare, native domestications of food plants, and the development of complex social systems caused revolutionary changes. But the coming of Europeans inaugurated a revolution of unimaginable proportions.

Here came horses, cattle, hogs, wheat, peaches, pears, gunpowder, glass, wagons, compasses, sextants, steel, generals, corporals, and Christian priests. The list is endless, the event mind-boggling. Unless we conceive of a modern-day invasion from outer space, there is nothing with which to compare it. It marked the beginning of the end of the old, classical desert ways of life. This Franciscan cross, beside a Spanish route of exploration and discovery, was found in 1991 by Rosemary Talley of the Museum of New Mexico.

CROSS

RIO ARRIBA COUNTY, NEW MEXICO
1991

152

AND THE WHITE MAN BROUGHT DISEASE. For every Native American killed deliberately by the invaders, hundreds more died of introduced European diseases: typhoid fever, smallpox, and others for which the Indians and Eskimos had no immunity. Ironically, more often than not these deadly scourges were passed on by foreigners who wished no harm.

In one way or another, "improving" the lives of the natives was the goal of many thousands of well-meaning whites. Indeed, in numerous respects these improvements have been so successful that few modern descendants of the first Americans would choose to go back to the rigors of ancient living. Still, the price has been high, as witnessed by these graves of Navajo men, women, and children, the victims of influenza and tuberculosis.

NAVAJO MISSION CHURCHYARD

SAN JUAN COUNTY, NEW MEXICO

1995

154

BIBLIOGRAPHY

Atkinson, Richard, 1981, *White Sands: Wind, Sand, and Time.* 44 pp. Globe, Arizona. Southwest Parks and Monuments Association.

Bean, Lowell John, 1978, "Cahuilla." In *Handbook of North American Indians,* vol. 8, *California,* ed. Robert Heizer, pp. 575–587. Washington, D.C. Smithsonian Institution.

Bean, Lowell John and Charles R. Smith, 1978, "Serrano." In *Handbook of North American Indians,* vol. 8, *California,* ed. Robert Heizer, pp. 570–574. Washington, D.C. Smithsonian Institution.

Benson, Lyman, 1981, *The Cacti of Arizona.* 218 pp. Tucson. University of Arizona Press.

Bowen, Thomas, 1983, "Seri." In *Handbook of North American Indians,* vol. 9, *The Southwest,* ed. Alfonso Ortiz, pp. 230–249. Washington, D.C. Smithsonian Institution.

Brown, David E., 1982, "Chihuahuan Desertscrub." In *Desert Plants,* vol. 4, nos. 1–7, *Biotic Communities of the American Southwest—United States and Mexico,* ed. David E. Brown, pp. 169–179. Tucson. University of Arizona Press.

Burt, W. H. and R. P. Grossenheider, 1964, *A Field Guide to the Mammals.* 284 pp. Cambridge, Massachusetts. The Riverside Press.

Chronic, Halka, 1984, *Roadside Geology of Arizona.* 314 pp. Missoula, Montana. Mountain Press Publishing.

Chronic, Halka, 1987, *Roadside Geology of New Mexico.* 255 pp. Missoula, Montana. Mountain Press Publishing.

Daubenmire, R., 1970, *Steppe Vegetation of Washington.* 131 pp. Pullman. Washington State University Press.

Dick-Peddie, W. A., 1993, *New Mexico Vegetation: Past, Present, and Future.* 144 pp. Albuquerque. University of New Mexico Press.

di Peso, Charles C. and Daniel S. Matson, eds. and trans., 1965, "The Seri Indians in 1692 as Described by Adamo Gilg, S.J." *Arizona and the West,* vol. 7, no. 1, pp. 33–56. Tucson. University of Arizona Press.

Dozier, Edward P., 1970, *The Pueblo Indians of North America.* 224 pp. New York. Holt, Rinehart and Winston.

Earle, W. Hubert, 1980, *Cacti of the Southwest Revised.* 209 pp. Scottsdale, Arizona. Published by the author.

Felger, Richard Stephen and Mary Beck Moser, 1985, *People of the Desert and Sea: Ethnobotany of the Seri Indians.* 435 pp. Tucson. University of Arizona Press.

Fiero, Bill, 1986, *Geology of the Great Basin.* 198 pp. Reno. University of Nevada Press.

Fowler, Catherine S., 1986, "Subsistence." In *Handbook of North American Indians,* vol. 11, *Great Basin,* ed. Warren L. D'Azevedo, pp. 64–97. Washington, D.C. Smithsonian Institution.

Fowler, Catherine S. and Sven Liljeblad, 1986, "Northern Paiute." In *Handbook of North American Indians,* vol. 11, *Great Basin,* ed. Warren L. D'Azevedo, pp. 435–465. Washington, D.C. Smithsonian Institution.

Fuller, Wallace H., 1975, *Soils of the Desert Southwest.* 102 pp. Tucson. University of Arizona Press.

George, Uwe, 1979, *In the Deserts of This Earth.* 309 pp. New York and London. Harcourt Brace Jovanovich.

Goodson, Gar, 1982, *Fishes of the Pacific Coast.* 267 pp. Stanford, California. Stanford University Press.

Hunt, Charles B., 1975, *Death Valley: Geology, Ecology, Archaeology.* 234 pp. Berkeley. University of California Press.

Jaeger, Edmund C., 1961, *Desert Wildlife.* 308 pp. Stanford, California. Stanford University Press.

Jennings, Jesse D., 1957, *Danger Cave.* 328 pp. Salt Lake City. University of Utah Press.

Jorgensen, Joseph P., 1980, *Western Indians: Comparative Environments, Languages, and Cultures of 172 Western American Indian Tribes.* 673 pp. San Francisco. W. H. Freeman.

Kelly, Isabel T. and Catherine S. Fowler, 1986, "Southern Paiute." In *Handbook of North American Indians,* vol. 11, *Great Basin,* ed. Warren L. D'Azevedo, pp. 368–397. Washington, D.C. Smithsonian Institution.

Kroeber, A. L., 1939, *Cultural and Natural Areas of Native North America.* 242 pp. Berkeley. University of California Press.

Lakits, Marie C., 1991, *Desert Drugstore: Traditional Solutions to the Stomach Ache.* 29 pp. Albuquerque. Unpublished manuscript on file in Clark Field Archive, University of New Mexico.

Larson, Peggy, 1977, *The Deserts of the Southwest.* 286 pp. San Francisco. Sierra Club Books.

Leland, Joy, 1986, "Population." In *Handbook of North American Indians,* vol. 11, *Great Basin,* ed. Warren L. D'Azevedo, pp. 608–619. Washington, D.C. Smithsonian Institution.

Liljeblad, Sven and Catherine S. Fowler, 1986, "Owens Valley Paiute." In *Handbook of North American Indians,* vol. 11, *Great Basin,* ed. Warren L. D'Azevedo, pp. 412–434. Washington, D.C. Smithsonian Institution.

Louw, G. N. and M. K. Seely, 1982, *Ecology of Desert Organisms.* 194 pp. New York. Longman, Inc.

McGinnies, William G., 1981, *Discovering the Desert*. 276 pp. Tucson. University of Arizona Press.

McGinnies, William G., Bram J. Goldman and Patricia Paylore, eds., 1977, *Deserts of the World*. 788 pp. Tucson. University of Arizona Press.

MacMahon, James A., 1985, *Deserts*, 638 pp. *The Audubon Society Nature Guides*. New York. Alfred A. Knopf, Inc.

McPhee, John, 1981, *Basin and Range*. 215 pp. New York. Farrar, Straus & Giroux.

Minckley, W. L. and David E. Brown, 1982, "Sonoran Oasis Forest and Woodlands." In *Desert Plants*, vol. 4, nos. 1–4, *Biotic Communities of the American Southwest — United States and Mexico*, ed. David E. Brown, p. 274. Tucson. University of Arizona Press.

Nabhan, Gary Paul, 1985, *Gathering the Desert*. 209 pp. Tucson. University of Arizona Press.

Noble, David Grant, 1993, *Ancient Ruins of the Southwest*. 218 pp. Flagstaff, Arizona. Northland Publishing Co.

Olin, George, 1977, *House in the Sun*. 236 pp. Phoenix. Southwest Parks and Monuments Association.

Porter, Stephen C., 1988, "Landscapes of the Last Ice Age in North America." In *Americans Before Columbus: Ice-Age Origins*, ed. Ronald C. Carlisle, pp. 1–24. Pittsburgh. University of Pittsburgh Press.

Reynolds, James F., 1986, "Adaptive Strategies of Desert Shrubs with Special Reference to Creosotebush (*Larrea tridentata* [DC] Cov.)." In *Pattern and Process in Desert Ecosystems*, ed. W. G. Whitford, pp. 19–49. Albuquerque. University of New Mexico Press.

Shimkin, Demitri B., 1947, "Wind River Shoshone Ethnogeography." *University of California Anthropological Records*, vol. 5, pp. 245–288. Berkeley. University of California Press.

Simmons, Marc, 1979, "History of Pueblo-Spanish Relations to 1821." In *Handbook of North American Indians*, vol. 9, *The Southwest*, ed. Alfonso Ortiz, pp. 178–193. Washington, D.C. Smithsonian Institution.

Steward, Julian H., 1938, *Basin-Plateau Aboriginal Sociopolitical Groups*. 346 pp. Bureau of American Ethnology Bulletin no. 120. Washington, D.C. Smithsonian Institution.

Stewart, Omer C., 1939, "The Northern Paiute Bands." *University of California Anthropological Records*, vol. 2, no. 3, pp. 127–149. Berkeley. University of California Press.

Thomas, David H., Lorann S. A. Pendleton and Stephen C. Cappannari, 1986, "Western Shoshone." In *Handbook of North American Indians*, vol. 11, *Great Basin*, ed. Warren L. D'Azevedo, pp. 262–283. Washington, D.C. Smithsonian Institution.

Turner, Raymond M., 1982, "Great Basin Desertscrub." In *Desert Plants*, vol. 4, nos. 1–4, *Biotic Communities of the American Southwest — United States and Mexico*, ed. David E. Brown, pp. 145–155. Tucson. University of Arizona Press.

Turner, Raymond M., 1982, "Mohave Desertscrub." In *Desert Plants*, vol. 4, nos. 1–4, *Biotic Communities of the American Southwest — United States and Mexico*, ed. David E. Brown, pp. 157–168. Tucson. University of Arizona Press.

Turner, Raymond M. and David E. Brown, 1982, "Sonoran Desertscrub." In *Desert Plants*, vol. 4, nos. 1–4, *Biotic Communities of the American Southwest — United States and Mexico*, ed. David E. Brown, pp. 181–221. Tucson. University of Arizona Press.

Vivian, R. Gwinn, 1990, *The Chacoan Prehistory of the San Juan Basin*. 523 pp. New York. Academic Press.

Whiteley, Peter M., 1988, *Deliberate Acts: Changing Hopi Culture Through the Oraibi Split*. 373 pp. Tucson. University of Arizona Press.

Whitford, W. G., ed. 1986, *Pattern and Process in Desert Ecosystems*. 139 pp. Albuquerque. University of New Mexico Press.

Windes, Thomas C., 1984, "A New Look at Population in Chaco

Canyon." In *Recent Research on Chaco Prehistory*, eds. W. James Judge and John D. Schelberg, pp. 75–88. Reports of the Chaco Center no. 8. Albuquerque. Division of Cultural Research, National Park Service.

Yetman, David, 1988, *Where the Desert Meets the Sea.* 177 pp. Tucson. Pepper Publishing.

Zwingle, Erla, 1993, "Ogallala Aquifer: Wellspring of the High Plains." *National Geographic,* vol. 183, no. 3, pp. 80–109. Washington, D.C. National Geographic Society.